ONE
CHURCH

"What does it mean to live as the Body of Christ? In *One Church*, Charles C. Camosy courageously names the full range of the maladies of division that plague our communities: generational, cultural, ethnic, political, social, and historical. He opens out in a gentle and practical way how the healing balm of love might enter into the nooks and crannies of daily interactions within Church life. With conversational ease and light-touch humor, Camosy thoughtfully guides his reader into a deeper appreciation and empathy for the complexity at the root of these challenging tensions. With real-life examples, he straddles the divisions to highlight the opportunities to learn, grow, build trust, and witness to the mutual love to which we are called as disciples of Christ."

Amy J. Uelmen
Director for Mission and Ministry
Georgetown Law School

"Camosy has a remarkable capacity to speak uncomfortable truths and make you laugh at the same time. While this book may be 'thin' and 'flat,' the content is anything but. Readers will leave with the ability to 'thicken' and 'add dimension' to common Catholic caricatures, opening the possibility for relationship, even in the midst of disagreement."

Ann M. Garrido
Author of *Let's Talk about Truth*

"Anyone who knows Camosy will know that his book is not a manual for compromising Catholic teaching in conversation and dialogue but rather a guide for how to engage in conversation and debate in a way that is less likely to reproduce already-polarized hostilities, which bear no fruit. This book suggests more likely ways of mitigating polarization that could ultimately generate a growing empathy and understanding for Catholic teaching, bearing fruit as Catholic teaching becomes a subject around which people feel more and more unified rather than polarized. But this takes strategic effort, and Camosy's book is here to help facilitate such effort. Highly recommended."

John C. Cavadini
McGrath-Cavadini Director
McGrath Institute for Church Life
University of Notre Dame

"I gobble up anything Camosy writes, but his latest book is especially tantalizing. Pope Benedict XVI remarked that we Catholics are usually more 'both–and' rather than 'either–or.' Camosy's book helps us achieve that. How timely this is during this synodality Pope Francis encourages with emphasis on trust, dialogue, and walking together."

Cardinal Timothy Dolan
Archbishop of New York

"Building bridges across political, ideological, religious, racial, and ethnic lines is a neglected and urgent imperative to advance the common good. Camosy offers challenging and wise strategies to begin with our own behaviors and attitudes rather than the shortcomings of others. Pope Francis calls us to listen and learn, to encounter and dialogue, and this timely book can help us follow these paths. Beginning with a little humility and humor, leading with what we are for, finding common ground around the Gospel, and keeping to principles of Catholic social teaching all offer ways forward in a wounded Church and polarized nation."

John Carr
Codirector of the Initiative on
Catholic Social Thought and Public Life
Georgetown University

"Charles C. Camosy's new work, *One Church*, is a very timely and critical work in this sound bite/internet age. Even in my graduate study days I observed that at the tables in the refectory of the graduate house of the North American College in Rome the seats were at times occupied by like-minded (eg, liberal/conservative) students with little variation daily. It was only when I became close friends with priests beyond that divide that I began to truly grow as priest and student in the Eternal City. I would try to sit at different tables each day and spend time with the priest students and others with whom I lived and studied with daily. If I had not made that effort my life would be very much different now. Some of those friends from those days 'across the divide' have stayed in my life to this day, along with becoming associated with the Focolare movement mentioned by Camosy specifically. Those sorts of divides sadly have become much more pronounced in this time of 'internet culture,' with the tendency to label everyone, as Camosy notes in his book. To begin anew and set ourselves on a firmer, stronger and more joyful path of faith and life in the Body of Christ, he shows us the way, especially with his five-step strategy to engage those whom the Lord in his providence sends our way."

Bishop Kevin Vann
Diocese of Orange

ONE
CHURCH

How to Rekindle Trust,
Negotiate Difference, and
Reclaim Catholic Unity

CHARLES C. CAMOSY

AVE MARIA PRESS AVE Notre Dame, Indiana

© 2022 by Charles C. Camosy

All rights reserved. No part of this book may be used or reproduced in any manner whatsoever, except in the case of reprints in the context of reviews, without written permission from Ave Maria Press®, Inc., P.O. Box 428, Notre Dame, IN 46556, 1-800-282-1865.

Founded in 1865, Ave Maria Press is a ministry of the United States Province of Holy Cross.

www.avemariapress.com

Paperback: ISBN-13 978-1-64680-152-7

E-book: ISBN-13 978-1-64680-153-4

Cover image © gettyimages.com.

Cover design by Kristen Hornyak Bonelli.

Text design by Christopher D. Tobin.

Printed and bound in the United States of America.

Library of Congress Cataloging-in-Publication Data is available.

Contents

Part I

FOUNDATIONS

Introduction

Here Comes Everybody

Is it too on-brand for a professor—especially a professor trying to write a practical field guide for the here and now—to begin by diving straight into history?

Well, I hope not. Our shared history is an essential part of what unites us as a Catholic Church.

But let's face it: our history tells us that deep divisions have been annoyingly persistent. From the very beginning, Peter and Paul—whose feast day we celebrate together on June 29 as pillars of the Church—went at it pretty hard over their fundamental differences. Paul even speaks of confronting Peter dramatically ("to his face"!) when the fisherman came to Antioch.

And this was just the beginning. Jerome and Augustine, two of the most brilliant minds of the Church, did not get along—and there are letters between them to prove it. As archbishop of Constantinople, St. John Chrysostom was deposed and banished. St. John of the Cross was kidnapped and held prisoner by fellow members of his own Carmelite order. For centuries it was Franciscans versus Dominicans and Jesuits versus just about everyone else. The sheer number of disputes testifies to how difficult it is to foster unity, even among people who share so much in common.

From 2000 to 2003 (before I was the kind of professor who, apparently, couldn't even wait four paragraphs before dropping names like "Chrysostom"), I taught a high school theology course called Catholic Social Teaching and Medical Ethics. This was my favorite course to teach because it combined social justice and pro-life perspectives and exposed my sixteen-year-old juniors to the fullness of the Church's teaching, across the whole left—right spectrum. I would go on to do a PhD in moral theology and bioethics at the University of Notre Dame with precisely this holistic, unifying vision in mind.

But it was my 2009 doctoral commencement at Notre Dame—the one at which President Obama spoke and was given an honorary degree—where I really began to confront just how dramatically divided the Church in the United States was. The Catholic blogosphere (an only-slightly-saner version of today's "weird Catholic Twitter") was ablaze with rancor and hate. Fox News had set up a special platform for extended live coverage leading up to the event. Letters to the editor on the *New York Times'* opinion page were coming fast and furious.

I found the whole blow-up so incredibly frustrating, not just because it needlessly divided a Catholic vision of the good but because there were so many people I deeply respected on multiple sides of the debate over whether a Catholic university such as Notre Dame should host and/or honor the then-president of the United States, given his extreme views on abortion. This tension was tearing at the very fabric of the Church in the United States.

That weekend, however, I resolved that as a Catholic theologian, bioethicist, and activist, I would work to show how the fullness of the Gospel and an authentic understanding of the Catholic faith can bring the kind of healing that comes from finding unity in our diversity.

Digitalizing Division

Professors are often accused of being deeply unrealistic about our ability to affect change, and I think most of us ought to admit that we are guilty as charged. Looking back, I can see now what a difficult goal I had set for myself. Facebook and Twitter were just coming on the scene, and these social media companies contributed dramatically to division in our Church—which became even worse over the next decade-plus. In the early days, I had hoped that platforms that made it so easy to share information could help expose Catholics to perspectives they wouldn't otherwise encounter. And while this does happen from time to time, the way social media companies have monetized our data at the service of their shareholders requires them to keep us scrolling our screens for as long as possible.

Exposing us to challenging ideas doesn't do that. Feeding us material that confirms our biases does.

If it was difficult to resist the us-versus-them tribalism that was already a problem in our Church, the ubiquity of social media (especially for young people who can't remember a time when things were different) has reinforced the righteousness of "our side" and our perception of how profoundly evil "the other side" is. These kinds of antagonistic binaries have become the primary ways we sort ourselves, even within the Church. We think of everything as an either-or: pro-life Catholics versus social justice Catholics; Francis bishops versus JPII bishops; guitar Mass versus Latin Mass; *Commonweal* versus *First Things*; woke Catholics versus MAGA Catholics. By the time this book is published, we will almost certainly have invented a new us-versus-them way to divide the Church.

The antagonistic binary imagination is so pernicious because instead of beginning with what unites us, it demands that we focus on what divides us. As a result, our identity is often defined not primarily in positive terms but rather in opposition to fellow Catholics. We identify far more with what—and who—we are against than with what we are for.

This is an utter scandal, especially for a Church led by the Christ who prayed that all may be one. It must be resisted with all that we have as a Church. And this starts by naming the sources of this kind of dangerously malformed imagination.

Idolatry and "The Big Sort"

Social media plays a significant role here—but it serves as more of an accelerant than actually providing the flame. The foundational problem is one of idolatry, especially political idolatry. The Gospel of Jesus Christ (um, spoiler alert) cannot be made to fit into any secular political party or agenda. But many US Catholics, it turns out, appear to have a stronger commitment to a secular political vision than to the Gospel as understood by Christ's Church. The success or failure of our political program or tribe often drives our ultimate concerns—and thus we imagine (or simply ignore) the Gospel with this narrow view in mind.

Enormous amounts of money are used by powerful people and institutions in order to achieve secular political objectives and goals. It is worth noting, however, that this same money often fuels Catholic figures and institutions—but only if they are clearly serving these same secular political objectives and goals.[1]

I write from firsthand experience. It is incredibly difficult to get serious funding from donors or grants from institutions when a project explicitly resists secular political agendas. It doesn't take too much imagination to think about a pitch like this going awry: "Uh, yes, ma'am. While the project I'm proposing supports a big-part-of-what-you-stand-for, I'm afraid we will also be trying to dismantle this other-big-part-of-what-you-stand-for." (*Cha-ching?* I don't think so.)

But with more money comes more resources and influence, including within the Church. Thus, the people and institutions within the Church that have the most influence tend to also be those that are most energetically serving secular political interests—since that's where the money is.

And when we think about the synergic way in which money, influence, politics, and social media work together we get what some have called "the big sort."[2] For all the talk about diversity in our current moment, most of us (of nearly all political persuasions) are choosing to live not only our virtual lives with those who are pretty much like us but also our actual, embodied lives. We sort ourselves into states, cities, and townships with people who are very much like us. We attend cultural events with people who are very much like us. Many of us even go parish shopping in order to worship with people who are very much like us.

And again, these kinds of relationships reinforce, rather than challenge, our biases. They keep us in a comfortable shell: a kind of safe space in which we rarely encounter views different from our own and where those in our orbit reassure us that others who hold such views are not worth engaging in any serious way.

"Thin" and "Flat"

In order to maintain these kinds of biases, we must flatten the views of "the other" into a thin, even dehumanizing, caricature. We must use lazy shorthand in order to maintain the kind of distance necessary for us to dismiss them without thinking. If we connect with the fullness of our perceived opponent's humanity, after all, we risk forming the kinds of genuine connections (and even affections!) that make people more difficult to discard. But there's no need to engage with people we flatten into "woke social-justice warriors," "out-of-touch bishops," "alt-right white supremacists," "lukewarm beige Catholics," "pro-lifers obsessed with pelvic issues," and so on.

Indeed, when we flatten our fellow Catholics into thin caricatures of who they really are—so fundamentally misguided
or even evil—it can become difficult to imagine how conversation is even possible, let alone desirable. Or even whether
it would be moral to legitimize a point of view by engaging
in dialogue in the first place. Perhaps the differences between
us are so great, and the views of "the other side" so manifestly
evil, that engagement must simply be abandoned in favor of
raw power plays.

Plus, these kinds of caricatures help affirm my identity in
opposition to the other.

The good people in the Church? Those worth engaging?
Well, it turns out they are pretty much like me. And by that,
I mean . . . well . . . *not them.*

A Fresh Approach

I'm going to try to do two primary things in this book to resist
this approach. First, I will show that many (if not most) of the
fellow Catholics we may put into these "thin" categories are
not who we think they are. We should not and will not paper
over real and significant differences—this book is absolutely
not about "happy talk." But at the same time, we must realize
that our differences are very often not what our social media
feeds and favorite magazines imagine them to be. Second, I
mean to provide a practical field guide for how to have difficult but genuinely productive conversations across our differences—modeling new ways to engage one another for a
broader culture addicted to destructive antagonism.

The key, as we will see in more detail, is embracing something that may seem utterly strange in our current moment
but is nevertheless profoundly Catholic: a willingness to be
united *in* our diversity. As a fanboy of the Focolare Movement's Catholic approach to unity, I've learned that we must
take a Trinitarian approach to dialogue, that is, an approach

that welcomes diversity with a kind of warm curiosity—knowing that we are united as a Church not in spite of our diversity, but because of it.[3] The very notion of relationship requires difference—unity-in-diversity—many parts, one body.

As a child of the 1980s, I was excited to see *Cobra Kai* become a bust-out hit on Netflix—and a whole new level of attention paid to the wisdom of one Mr. Miyagi, Daniel's mentor from the original *Karate Kid* films. In the original movie, Daniel is having problems with his girlfriend, Ali Mills, when Miyagi comes across a photo of the two of them together and says, "Look good together. Different, but same."

The relationship between Daniel and Ali is instructive for the relationship we need to have as Church. Catholics must learn to see each other as different but same. We are many distinct parts but united as the Body of Christ—the Church—through our Baptism. We are all brothers and sisters in Christ. In a very real sense, we are family.

But let's have some real talk: Almost all families have substantial differences. If your family was without dramatic disagreements, and even terrible fights, then more power to you. This is not the experience of the overwhelming majority of families. But grounded families rest assured that they remain a family throughout it all. What unites them is stronger than even their worst arguments. Their foundational love never wavers, and they are willing to suffer with their family members through bad times at the service of that love. And as we will see throughout this book, a willingness to suffer with (and for!) our family members in the Church is essential for the unity Christ asks for in the Church.

In my experience, humor is an important tool families use to work through their difficulties. My parents and siblings made sure to poke fun at my way-too-self-assuredness (something that seems to be in every professor's job description) as a way of keeping me in check. Given my critique of the "thin" and "flat" caricatures mentioned above, readers who have looked at the table of contents might wonder about my own use of the very thin labels I just criticized for most of the chapter titles. Part of this is, frankly, a bit of poking fun at fellow family members and addressing a difficult reality with humor. Maybe you will find yourself, or a significant part of yourself, in one or more of these groups. I certainly do.[4]

But please also take notice of the *subtitles* of these chapters. Sometimes families can unfairly focus on the caricatures that can't accurately capture the fullness of who we are because they are too "thin" and too "flat." Many of us, no doubt, have struggled to break out of the perception our parents or siblings had of us as children.

Truth be told, it is a perfectly natural part of ourselves to categorize others; we do it without thinking as an evolutionary part of human reality and an especially deep part of ourselves when it comes to threat assessment. But when one combines this deep part of our nature as *Homo sapiens* with what I've already described as the idolatrous influence of secular politics, money, and social media, well, we've got something to very clearly and intentionally resist. And we do that successfully by focusing on the full reality of our brothers and sisters in Christ.

I write this book as a field guide for doing precisely this.

Mission Possible

Despite the pitfalls that await a project like this (one friend who heard I was writing a book like this noted that I was doing it "on the eve of what might be a formal schism with the Church in Germany"), I do so with confidence that the goal of unity-in-diversity can be achieved. Some of this confidence might be my personality (see above), and a good deal comes from learning about history, but much of it comes from my own experiences. I have personally been all over the political and theological map and know well why someone might locate themselves in one place or another.

But I've also been an unceasing advocate for dialogue and exchange across difference with some of the unlikeliest bedfellows imaginable. That includes people like Peter Singer, a professor of bioethics at Princeton University, someone who has made a career by declaring a frontal assault on the value I hold most dear: the sanctity and fundamental equality of every human life. Among other things, he and I were the founding coorganizers of an international conference trying to find new ways to think and speak about abortion.

I've led Catholic conversation projects with everyone from high-powered theologians to my local fellow parishioners. I've facilitated dialogues between pro-life and animal rights activists. I've been part of academic projects bringing together Catholics, Muslims, and secular thinkers on medicine and bioethics. As a board member of Democrats for Life, I have witnessed both the struggles (at the national level where the polarization is profound) and the successes (at the state level where people tend to engage each other as people) of bringing the fullness of a "whole life" or "consistent life" vision to those who are skeptical. I've been blessed to write pieces for outlets all over the political and theological spectrum: from the *New York Times* to the *New York Post* and from *Commonweal* to *First Things*.

Whether I'm having an exchange with a newspaper editor, a fellow parishioner, an academic, a legislator, or a neighbor, I can tell you plainly: *the principles and strategies laid out in the next chapter work.* They are sometimes difficult to execute—and they may not work in every single instance—but overall and in the main, they are extremely effective in finding and fostering unity. And once we have the principles and strategies in place, we can explore how to employ them in specific exchanges we have with our fellow Catholics—especially those with whom we find such exchanges difficult.

This book is a field guide to having those conversations. The real learning comes from doing the work of dialogue.

Here's to the doing!

1

Getting to Unity-in-Diversity

The dignity of the human person as the divine image-bearer must be our starting point for dialogue. We hear this statement so often in Catholic circles that it can become a cliché we may zoom right past without thinking about it very much. Sometimes we fail to think about the dignity of those with whom we are having a difficult conversation—even when the disagreement is over what the dignity of the human person means or demands! Speaking as a dyed-in-the-wool Cubs fan, one of the most difficult things my faith teaches me is that even Cardinals fans are made in the image and likeness of God.

And very often it goes well beyond losing sight of the dignity of our perceived opponent; sometimes their dignity is the very thing explicitly being questioned or attacked. Descriptions of fellow Catholics as "monstrous" or "diabolical" are, unfortunately, a dime a dozen in what passes for Catholic discourse today in the United States.

But here's an uncomfortable truth: it can be extremely difficult to keep the inherent dignity of the person with whom we profoundly disagree at the front of our minds. Though fear and anger can blind us to our own biases and cut us off from a real exchange with someone else, there may be good reasons to be profoundly angry with a fellow Catholic. This should be fully honored, while at the same time acknowledging that the fundamental reality of the person in front of us is the starting point for any serious exchange. No matter what they think, how they treat us, or where their baseball loyalties lie, they are made in the image and likeness of God.

And this demands something of us—regardless of how uncomfortable it may be.

Love First

Again, one thing should give us confidence going into this: the Church has been dealing with these kinds of challenges for two thousand years and, with the help of the Holy Spirit, has developed a huge arsenal of spiritual and practical tools. Some are as simple as they are powerful.

When I'm caught in the midst of a difficult exchange, one in which I'm prone to forget that the person with whom I'm engaging is a Temple of the Holy Spirit, I remember the great gift the Focolare has given me in the following exhortation: *Be the first to love.* While this plays upon my unreasonably competitive nature, it opens up space for genuine dialogue across difference. Loving first is important at a foundational level because it is what we owe anyone who bears the image and likeness of God. In a very real sense, when we choose to reduce, attack, and demean the dignity of the person in front of us, we choose to attack and demean God's image as well.

That is true regardless of which human being we fail to love. But very often the victim is a fellow baptized Catholic. Again, the contemporary world very often trains us to see fellow Catholics first as allies or foes in relation to secular political goals. Is this a MAGA person, or are they a "social justice warrior"? Is this person an LGBTQ+ ally, or are they "homophobic"? And so on.

As disciples of Jesus, we are called to allow the grace of Christ and of his Church to shape us into those who are the first to love our perceived opponent. That can happen only when we see them through a very different kind of lens. Before we identify a person in any other way, we must first see them as a family member—a brother or sister in Christ—whom we are called to love before we are called to do anything else.

This, to say the least, is not rewarded in the secular world and especially not on social media—both of which obscure the dignity of those we are taught to dismiss as merely "the other side." In both political and virtual discourse (and *especially* in virtual discourse about politics), our perceived opponents are depersonalized such that we are almost never confronted with their humanity.

Remember being called into the principal's office of a Catholic school? (Bonus points if that principal was a nun or priest!) What I'm about to say may feel similar to that, though if it makes you feel any better, I don't exempt myself from the criticism I'm about to make.

As Catholics we should know better—but very often we don't do better. Especially on social media, our first reaction is often to attack, disparage, and define by opposition—when we ought to demonstrate respect and even reverence for the shared humanity of our perceived opponents. One way to resist the world's practices here is to be super intentional about following Christ's command to genuinely pray for them. It may feel (temporarily) good to "own the libs/cons"—to get the high fives and bro-love from "your side." But it should go without saying that the very thing that is implied in owning someone in this sense does not start with their dignity as a fellow being created in the image of God. And it almost never arrives at a mutual sense of shared dignity arising from a Gospel-centered love.

But even when we manage to think explicitly about our conversation partners as fellow family members in the Church, the challenges do not magically disappear. Indeed, in some ways they become more complex. The fact that "familiarity breeds contempt" is one reason there are so many challenges in family life—and this is certainly the case with our Catholic family. We may feel anger or even rage that makes it difficult to imagine how an exchange might go. Or we may not want to validate someone who holds views we abhor by engaging with them.

But, again, they are dignified in the same way "our side" is, whether we choose to acknowledge it or not. They are dignified in the most profound way possible: they bear the divine image and are temples of the Holy Spirit. This is an essential and fundamental truth of the Catholic faith.

Do you find yourself getting in your own way when it comes to being the first to love?

Well, good news: there's a virtue for that.

Listening with Humility

Most of us can think back to a time when we held opinions or views quite different from those we do now. (At one point in my life, for instance, I used to think that wearing spandex shorts was a good idea.) It is overwhelmingly likely that, at some point in the future, we will see some things quite differently than we do now as well. This insight should be enough for us to reserve the right to change our minds in light of a genuine exchange with someone who thinks differently.

When we look back at how we have changed, often we can point to a particular encounter with a person that led to that change. Usually, that encounter was unexpected: God has this way of putting people on our path to lead us where we need to go on our journey of faith.

Not everyone we encounter is such a person, however. (Whichever person in junior high convinced me to wear the spandex shorts was definitely *not* doing this.) In fact, as anyone who looks back into their dating past usually knows all too well, we are often terrible judges of character. We may think we know everything that's relevant and important about someone we are dating, but more often than not, we don't. That's why we must engage in careful, prayerful discernment about whether a given person is in fact leading us closer to God.

Authentic discernment requires cultivating the virtue of humility by listening to God through prayer, listening to our own hearts (which God often reveals to us through prayer), and listening—genuinely listening—to the human person with whom we are engaging. Only then can we put our own biases, agendas, and expectations aside and allow God's Holy Spirit, through the person we are encountering, the freedom to work in our lives.

As Jesus said to Nicodemus, "The wind blows where it wills, and you can hear the sound it makes, but you do not know where it comes from or where it goes; so it is with everyone who is born of the Spirit" (Jn 3:8). We need the kind of humility that opens up a space for God and God's image-bearers to move us, sometimes in an unexpected—and perhaps uncomfortable—direction.

Too often, however, the kind of listening we usually do is akin to the way my teenagers "listen" to my explanations for why I'm cutting their screen time. They are listening for weakness or contradiction. "But Dad, you had a different standard just last week!" "But Dad, you use your phone way more than we do!" "But Dad, you say you are doing this for my benefit, but how can it be for my benefit *if I have no friends*?!"

The current discourse (especially on social media) trains us how to listen for a mistake or gap to name and exploit. This is the opposite of listening with the humility that makes it possible for us to love first, to allow the encounter with the person to bring us closer to God and God's will for us. What we've become accustomed to doing reinforces our own biases and closes us off from having them genuinely challenged and allowing those challenges to change our minds.

I'm all for a good argument. Having an exchange about gaps in logical reasoning is super important. Plus, in the right context, a good argument can be fun and build bonds of love between people who already know and trust each other. But this is not the place to *begin* an encounter with another person. A productive argument is possible only after one has acknowledged and committed to respect the fullness of another's humanity.

Especially when it comes to discourse on sensitive topics and ones that typically happen on social media, a lack of listening (again, related to a lack of genuine encounter with the fullness of a real person) leads us to reduce a point of view to something we don't like about who they are. For example, "His view about Y says so much about his white privilege." Or, "Her view about X comes from her trying to justify her own lifestyle!"

Still less should we build fences by using thin and flat labels to describe our perceived opponents. It may give us a quick dopamine hit to score a rhetorical point, especially online, and watch the affirmation from our side flow in. But using phrases such as "anti-science" or "pro-birth" boxes someone into a thin caricature that can then be dismissed as obviously wrong or even evil. And while the substantive issues gestured at by references to lifestyle, privilege, science, and the significance of birth may end up playing a role in a love-centered exchange of different ideas, we must never, ever reduce a person into a thin caricature. Doing so misunderstands and even disrespects the kind of creature God created them to be.

Instead, we must strive to listen with the kind of humility that allows a "thick" story of who a person is and why they hold the views they do to emerge—even though this may challenge (rather than simply confirm) our biases.

Thick Is Greater than Thin and Dimensional Is Greater than Flat

It's often a struggle to genuinely engage the fullness of another human being. It can be difficult to be open to the "thickness" of his or her perspective because it forces us to go beyond a quick and dirty label and enter into the reality of someone we may feel more comfortable dismissing as obviously wrong or evil. Recall the flattening out of complex people into "woke social justice warriors" or "alt-right white supremacists."

But another major reason it can be difficult to avoid substituting caricatures for people is that it takes hard work over a period time to build a real relationship, not just a virtual one, with strangers we will never meet, and not merely an acquaintance with fellow parishioners. Building a relationship of encounter and hospitality with someone else is the only way to get the thick and multidimensional version of who they are. Over time, we learn the answers to the kinds of questions that give us a deeper understanding of who they are. What is their history? What have they been through? What experiences have they had that we have not? Might they have reasons for taking a position that we disagree with or haven't thought about? Is their view on one issue (where we disagree) connected to their view on another issue (where we agree) in ways we couldn't see before?

Again, there is an important place for hashing out arguments and evidence, for speaking and writing precisely and carefully. But there is something uniquely important and revealing about an embodied, in-person encounter. And making a physical place for someone, perhaps even in one's home or other personal space in the spirit of hospitality, increases the capacity to thicken the encounter in ways I don't think we fully understand or appreciate. Phrases like "the eyes are the window to the soul"—along with references to "vibe" and "body language"—hint at some of what goes on in an embodied encounter. In an embodied encounter, we have much more access to the fullness of who someone is (and they to us!)—and in ways that surely elude us if all we have are words on a page or screen or if we see them only through Zoom or video platforms. Ultimately, though we experience it countless times in our lives, what happens in an embodied encounter is a mystery that defies rational explanation.

And there is something deeply theological here. The Father sends the Son to us through the Spirit *not* by means of words on a page or even as an image. As important as words and images can be, God came to us *by means of a physical, embodied encounter.* Catholic life is an ongoing encounter with a God who became a human being in the flesh through the Blessed Mother Mary. The first Christians got to encounter Jesus in a special way in history, but Christ left us a way to experience him by means of another kind of physical, embodied encounter: the Eucharist. Because of the Eucharist, we connect to Christ in a deeper, more authentic, and more intimate way.

During the COVID-19 pandemic, many Catholics felt distant from our faith, not just because many couldn't attend Mass but also because we missed the physical, embodied, sacramental encounter with the Lord through the Eucharist. The intense feeling I had going to Mass (and especially getting in the Communion line) after so many months of not being able to be present was unlike anything I had ever experienced. It was so clear that I had missed this embodied experience on a fundamental level. Though I had watched it many, many times on a virtual live stream, the mysterious difference of the embodied encounter was as real as it gets. Again, it is a mystery, but as with other kinds of physical, embodied encounters, we just know there is something different about that kind of relationship.

Our world is pushing us away from these kinds of embodied relationships. Our faith, however, is drawing us toward them. Again, the temptation here is for us to see others as perceived opponents and dismiss them without ever having to take them seriously as people. But we must push back against a throwaway culture that discards people and insist instead on a culture of encounter and hospitality that reveals the thickness and fullness of another's perspective—especially when we don't see eye to eye.

The Cost of Encounter

I want to emphasize that mere "happy talk" accomplishes nothing. We should be clear-eyed about what I've just proposed might mean for us: radical discomfort. It might mean engaging with a Catholic who voted for Donald Trump or one who identifies with they/them pronouns. It might mean singing a few Mass responses in Latin or calling young children into the sanctuary for the homily at the "family Mass." It might mean cultivating precisely the kinds of difficult encounters from which our sorted, categorized culture is designed to shield us, and not only with the intention of scoring points or changing others' points of view.

But as I recently wrote in my "Purple Catholicism" column for the Religion News Service, the Focolare Movement reminds us that Christ-centered love means dialoguing into the pain of "Jesus forsaken," that is, the dying Christ who felt the terrible pain of being abandoned by the Father while on the Cross.[1] It means choosing the self-emptying love required to have difficult encounters and to make those encounters fruitful. It means being vulnerable to the reality of someone with views that not only offend us but also make us deeply uncomfortable. Uniting ourselves with Jesus forsaken by living out a culture of encounter and hospitality can blast apart the protective shells guarding our safe spaces and open us to the fullness of the reality—often a painful reality—of those with whom we find conversation difficult. It can also blast apart those same barriers in the person we are engaging in dialogue.

And this need not be only or even mostly a fearful or negative experience. I can't help but think of Pope Francis recently urging us to live with the *joy* of someone who has the stigmata.[2] Yes, the kind of exchange and dialogue I'm proposing here can be deeply uncomfortable, but with the right attitude, it can also be joyful, life-giving, and exciting.

This kind of Christian adventure requires us to cast out into the deep. Here I'm moved to invoke J. R. R. Tolkien and especially his image of Bilbo Baggins finding the courage to leave the safe space of his hobbit hole and embrace the "Tookish" side of himself. Tolkien describes it this way in *The Hobbit*:

> Then something Tookish woke inside of him, and he wished to go and see the great mountains, and hear the pine-trees and the waterfalls, and explore the caves, and wear a sword instead of a walking stick.

Far too often, US Catholics find ourselves trapped by our comfortable, safe, sorted lives. And while there is nothing wrong with being comfortable, safe, and sorted, when that kind of life becomes a dangerous idol—one that keeps us from being able to encounter the fullness of our fellow Catholics—then it is time to burst out of the door of our hobbit holes, make for the Inn of the Prancing Pony, and see what adventures God has in store for us.

Paying Attention to Power

Mike Tyson is not traditionally invoked as a font of wisdom. But perhaps the most powerful puncher in the history of boxing did get one thing profoundly correct when he was quoted as saying, "Everyone has a plan until they get punched in the mouth." In a variation on that theme, we might also say that it is all well and good to have the kind of plan I've articulated thus far—but if we fear being punched in the mouth or have been punched in the mouth in the past, then maybe the plan isn't worth all that much.

We must pay close attention to how power is function-ing in our relationships. Power is often at the heart of why someone articulates the view they do—and also, significantly, why someone may be afraid to articulate a more authentic position. A good dialogue must think about power in the life of our conversation partner, in our own lives, and in the rela-tionship between them and us. And it is only when we enter into the fullness of their "thick" reality—only when we start with loving them as a child of God and brother or sister in Christ—that we can really discern how power is functioning.

And here we can start with a few questions for ourselves:

- Do we feel free to say what we really believe to be true?

- What orthodoxies are present that we do not feel free to challenge?

- Who might, through the use of power, enforce these orthodoxies in ways that could harm us or those close to us if we do not conform?

- How might our answers to these questions limit our ability to really listen and engage?

We can then ask similar questions about the person we're engaging and think about how it might impact their ability to listen and engage:

- Are we getting the full and unvarnished truth?

- Might there be important things that aren't being said or important context that isn't being offered?

And then there's the power dynamics of the relationship between us:

- Are there things that cannot be said, or at least cannot be said clearly and honestly, because of these power dynamics?
- Or even because of the *perceived* power dynamics?

But even as we attempt to answer these questions, we should also focus on how power is functioning as a gatekeeper of the facts to which we have access. And here's a quick (only somewhat tongue-in-cheek) question in light of that concern. Who do you think has more power in their particular social contexts: (1) Emperor Palpatine, Lord Vader, and Grand Admiral Thrawn or (2) Mark Zuckerberg, Jack Dorsey, and Sundar Pichai?

Companies such as Facebook, Twitter, and Google have used profit-generating algorithms to limit the facts and perspectives we encounter on a day-to-day basis and procure a kind of power that was unimaginable only a decade ago. We can be intentional about resisting them, but it is difficult, even for those with the best intentions and strongest wills, given how our access to information is structured by these companies. Something similar can be said about the power that political and activist organizations (and allied media mouthpieces, such as cable "news" and talk radio) have in cultivating our comfortable, politically insulated hobbit holes. Awareness of how this kind of power is functioning must also be front and center.

Once a love-centered dynamic has been established, the way political power in particular is functioning should be named and actively resisted. Part of what should unite Catholics participating in an exchange across difference is our common commitment to Christ and his Church—a commitment that absolutely must not mirror the commitments of secular political activists in the early twenty-first-century United States.

If a Catholic has views that line up neatly with Fox News, MSNBC, the *Wall Street Journal*, or *Mother Jones*, then something has gone very wrong. The Holy Spirit cannot be made to fit into contemporary secular political categories, and therefore any authentically Catholic perspective should expect to have serious distance from them. The fact that so many US Catholics do line up neatly with these perspectives—or at least feel they cannot challenge them without getting punched in the mouth—gives us good reason to think about the power of our political discourse to push Catholics to idolatrously prioritize a secular ideology over the Gospel.

The Gospel, of course, turns the secular world's idea of power on its head. Jesus tells us that the last shall be first and the first shall be last. Those who try to save their life will lose it, and those who are willing to lose their life will save it. Jesus was at his most powerful when he was hanging on the Cross and felt abandoned by the Father, when he felt the most powerless. Authentic power comes from dying to self, and true leadership shows itself in service, both literally and figuratively washing others' feet.

Catholics pursuing this kind of disruptive power will not only be much better at diagnosing how a different view of power is functioning in our exchanges. They will also choose to engage with their perceived opponents in ways that upend typical power dynamics. Again, they will embrace Jesus forsaken and choose to engage with humble listening.

Breaking the Antagonistic Binary

It is bad enough that so many Catholics have sold out their faith to the idol of secular politics on both the right and the left. But think for a moment about the *particular* secular politics in the United States—driven as it is by antagonistic us-versus-them binaries. To the extent that our identity comes from adherence to such politics, it will be near impossible to find unity-in-diversity. Again, the nature of this kind of binary way of seeing the world pits people against each other. A person's very identity comes from the fact that we exist in a polarized, antagonistic relationship with "the other side."

We cannot seek unity-in-diversity, in this context, without losing ourselves in the process.

Many Catholics have adopted the habit characteristic of our secular politics in which we identify more with what we are against than with what we are for. Our hopelessly simplistic two-party system focuses people with very different convictions into coalitions that, for instance, ask us to shove seventeen different and often incoherent positions into the platform of a single party. (What does MAGA-style nationalism have in common with neoconservatism, anyway? What does a focus on unions and the working class have to do with woke capitalism? And so on.)

In such a case, the glue that holds our secular political coalitions together is obviously not rooted in a common vision of the common good. Rather, it is derived from a cut-and-paste antagonism toward "the other side" that unites the party. While one may not agree with much of what the elephant or the donkey stands *for* these days, he or she may like the fact the party fights *against* the kinds of people we've labeled and dismissed as white supremacists or social justice warriors—people on whom our very identity relies on being evil.

This is why it is so important for Catholics to fight as hard as we can to remove ourselves from this idolatrous political mindset and imagination and to stop applying the same destructive paradigm to nonpolitical matters of how we practice the faith. If we are going to get to unity-in-diversity, to diversity-in-unity, we must lead with a positive vision of what we are for rather than focusing on what we are against. And maybe we can lead strategically with certain carefully chosen things that we are for. What ideas and values could serve as windows for us to peer more deeply into the reality of another person and discover goals and values we might have in common? How can these common goals and values be used as a door for us to enter into the beginnings of a dialogue about matters of perceived disagreement?

We've already emphasized our overarching common brotherhood or sisterhood in Christ. But figuring out what we might call our "Catholic least common denominators" can provide an important foundation for getting the most out of our exchanges.

Some readers may remember an ancient time in which a good number of us decided that it was a good idea to wear colored rubber bands on our wrists. Maybe you recall the "LiveStrong" yellow ones devoted to cancer research that then proliferated into every color and cause under the sun? Back in the day, I had a green one that said "vegetarian" and a blue one that said "pro-life." If I'm honest, at least part of the reason I wore them was that I got caught up in the silly virtue-signaling of that time. But I also did it because I wanted to signal common ideological ground to a wide range of people. If some could agree with me on pro-life, that was enough for a large number of people to take me seriously on other matters. If others could see I was concerned about the welfare of animals, that was enough for a very different set of folks to take me seriously on other matters as well. And it also troubled our secular political and ideological binary in ways I found too delicious to pass up!

It should also be said that the vision offered by our antagonistic this-or-that imagination absolutely does not describe where Americans are politically. If you choose four people at random in the United States, about one identifies as a Republican, one identifies as a Democrat, and two identify as independents. Most people are not ideologues. Indeed, most are part of an "exhausted majority" looking for a different way to engage.[3]

Furthermore, we are currently in the midst of a major political realignment in which what the two major parties stand for is neither stable nor clear. The typical lines of demarcation—focused as they have been on "big versus small government" and "business/corporate interests versus those of the little guy"—have been largely erased over the last decade. What is coming next isn't at all clear, which means Catholics should be even more confident in rejecting a tired, played-out, hopelessly simplistic binary imagination.

Getting to Authentic Disagreement

OK, let's say our attempts to engage in a difficult conversation have followed everything laid out to this point. We started with the God-given dignity of our conversation partner; we've engaged in humble listening that embraces Jesus forsaken; we've rejected the typically thin and flat caricatures and instead attempted to enter into the thickness of their perspective; and we've mapped out the power dynamics and led with what we are for (not with what we're against), breaking the antagonistic binary and finding significant common ground.

But there's still disagreement. Maybe even very serious, profound disagreement.

Now what?

First of all, do not be surprised. The ideas, principles, and techniques I've outlined above will help us steer clear of certain classic challenges. However, we are by no means able to avoid all honest disagreements. Far from it. Indeed, in some ways what we are doing is what's necessary for *having a productive disagreement at all*. I always tell my students that reaching actual disagreement—especially in our current culture—is an achievement that requires real work.

We must honor our differences; it does no one any good to paper over them. But at the same time, we must make it absolutely clear that our disagreement always comes from a place of love—not the condescending "I-know-what's-best" love but rather the love of a sibling or friend who can tell you that you have something caught in your teeth or that you've gotten into the habit of pulling for the St. Louis Cardinals again. Communicating that we are willing to humbly listen and reserve the right to change our minds creates even more space for authentic disagreement. Our discussion partner can trust that we are operating in good faith and that we will disagree with the full substance of their position, not merely an impoverished caricature of it. We will listen to them as people with all the dignity God has given them, and not just to poke holes in the views they hold.

Notice, however, that humble disagreement in love does not require us to stop trying to be persuasive. Again, this is far from the case. If a family member or friend (or in this case a fellow Catholic) is in error or has overlooked something that is hurting them, then trying to persuade them of this fact is the loving thing to do.

The approach we took through humble listening gives them permission to do the same for us. This dynamic, of course, is rarely the kind of thing that develops overnight. Often the best we can hope for at first is that seeds are planted that grow as the relationship develops over time and more exchanges take place. We should not expect some kind of thunderous, paradigm-shifting "Aha!" moment. Rather, we should plan to accompany those with whom we find con-versation difficult on a journey—a journey that, if it follows the path laid out here, is likely to change all those involved in significant ways.

And if we journey long enough to gain something like clarity about what is going on, it may be that our differences turn out not to be substantive disagreements at all but more about points of emphasis. The Church is one Body, but it has many different parts. Differences are *required* for there to be a relationship in the first place. And the differences between various Catholics are often profound gifts to the Church. It is good and necessary that we have arms and legs and backs and shoulders and heads and bellies. This kind of unity-in-diversity is one of the great strengths of a Catholic Church that exemplifies the words of James Joyce, the great Irish poet, who once said of the Church, "Here comes everybody."

But here's a very important point: the "unity" part of unity-in-diversity is mystical and transcendent. It comes from sharing a common Baptism and from a common commitment to the true claims and teachings of the Church into which one has been baptized. This gives us numerous common starting points (such as the dignity of the human person created by God in his image and likeness and that our salvation is dependent on how we treat the least among us) that are necessary for an exchange between Catholics to get us off the ground.

What it means to be unified as the Catholic Church cannot be determined by, say, a majority vote of how self-identified US Catholics feel about any given topic in the early part of the twenty-first century. Unity in the Church is unity with the Church universal, in the sense that it includes not just those outside our national borders but also those who have gone before us in the Communion of Saints and those who will come after us as well. At the same time, however, true Catholic unity is too deep and expansive to be limited to a kind of slavish, unthinking adherence to every single utterance of one's local bishop or every word of every document written by every single pope who ever lived.

We will explore more about these matters in specific contexts in the chapters that follow, but it is safe to say that what unity-in-diversity in the Church means can be complex and even unclear. Thus the need for—you guessed it—humble listening while reserving the right to change our minds in light of where God is leading us.

The Holy Spirit blows where it will.

This Is a Field Guide

Each chapter that follows is outlined with six steps that translate into workable principles for increased dialogue. They are labeled like this:

- The Thin Caricature
- What Is in Our Hearts?
- A Story That Thickens
- What Are the Gifts and Truths Being Proclaimed?
- What Are the Challenges?
- Opportunities for Unity-in-Diversity

Even if we follow these steps and practice the principles they describe, we should (again) expect serious disagreement with our fellow Catholics. This has been the way of things from the very beginnings of the Church—and between some of the most holy people who have ever practiced the faith. Remember that this is a practical field guide for having *difficult* conversations with our fellow Catholics, especially (but not only) with those we might think of as our opponents or adversaries. The principles and techniques will not work every single time, and we may well run into people who refuse to play by the same rules or even operate in bad faith. But, again, I speak from personal experience when I say that these principles and techniques work. They work even when the disagreement is white-hot and the probability of a genuine exchange seems quite low.

I've tried to lay out the principles and techniques in a way that hints at how they could apply to difficult conversations in the Church. Perhaps you've already been thinking about people in your own life with whom some of these ideas might work. But I was intentionally abstract here at the beginning in order to set up very specific applications for each of the groups discussed in the rest of the book. So, if you want practical, real-life applications—well, hold onto your hats and keep reading.

In each of the chapters that follow, I'll apply the general principles I've outlined in chapter 1 to a specific group in the Church with which some significant percentage of Catholics find conversation difficult. In pursuit of this goal, I will do all or most of the following:

- Name the thin and flat caricature we may have attached to a group in the Church, but then invite the reader to listen with humility as I attempt to thicken out their shared perspective

- Tell a story or anecdote that thickens out and gives dimension to our understanding of this group's members

- Discuss the unique and valuable gifts each group brings to the Church

- Identify some of the challenges each group offers for Catholics with a different perspective

- Suggest opportunities for moving toward unity-in-diversity

My deep hope is that many Catholics will apply this field guide in parishes, schools, and other Catholic institutions toward building unity in our incredibly diverse US Church. I believe that we can come to a place in which we can say of our fellow Catholics (including those who we may think often get important things wrong):

"We are different but the same."

Part II

GENERATIONAL DIVIDES

2

The Spirit-of-Vatican-II Boomer

I.e., "The In-Their-Bones Catholic"

1. The Thin Caricature

I can imagine a reader coming to this chapter's title and asking, "Um, Charlie? Didn't you just finish telling us not to caricature people and groups with phrases and labels like—oh, I don't know, *spirit-of-Vatican-II Boomer*? What in the name of lack of self-awareness is going on here?"

Well, what's going on here (and in every other following chapter) is an attempt to highlight different kinds of family members in our midst. We also need to become more aware of the caricatures we (and others) sometimes use to go along with a dismissive phrase or label. Believe me, in the next few pages, we will be "thickening" our understanding of folks who may fall into this group. But we're also going to have a bit of good-natured fun with our fellow members of the Catholic family along the way!

And with that in mind, I'll begin with a joke I've heard that upholds the thin and flat caricature.

Now, "Good Pope John" XXIII showed up at the
Pearly Gates after his death. But a puzzled St.
Peter could not find him "in the books" as it were.
Pope John, getting a bit worried and agitated, said,
"Look me up under my birth name . . . Roncalli . .
. RONCALLI!"

When St. Peter still came up empty, Good
Pope John insisted that he speak with the apostle's
Supervisor.

So, St. Peter called up the Holy Spirit who
responded to Good Pope John with a generous,
"How can I help you, good sir?"

Good Pope John, now jumping up and down at
this point given that even the Supervisor failed to
recognize him, said, "I *must* be on the list! I'm the
pope! John XXIII! I just called the Second Vatican
Council!"

To which the Holy Spirit went ashen and said,
"Oh yeah . . . I was supposed to show up to that."

If you remember The Beatles on *The Ed Sullivan Show*, tie-
dye, Woodstock, or the first time you heard the Mass offered
in English, you probably do so with some nostalgia and affection. And if you don't remember those things, well, there's a
decent chance you're irritated by those who do. But even if you
are quite sympathetic toward this group, this joke highlights
quite well a central thin caricature that some have: that those
Catholics who talk about the "spirit of Vatican II" don't really
have the *Holy* Spirit in mind.

What they have instead is the cultural spirit of the US Baby
Boomer or, more generally, radical individualism, selfishness,
anti-institutionalism, hostility toward authority, sexual lib-
eration, a suspicion of tradition and traditional practices, a
modernist approach to art and beauty, a reductionist account
of the enchanted world, and so on. By abandoning the traditional content of Catholic faith, the spirit-of-Vatican-II Baby

Boomers (or so the caricature goes) paved the way for a vacuous, nicey-nice-feel-good, dumbed-down approach to the spiritual life.

You know, the kind of approach to catechesis in which a young Catholic is asked "to imagine and draw God if God were a tree."

And this critique has been around for decades. But another one has been on the rise in recent years as the Baby Boomers have gotten older, one that mirrors the larger "OK, Boomer" critique in the culture more broadly. The basic idea is that this group is simply old and out of touch. They still imagine themselves to be hip and on the cutting edge, pushing boundaries in the Church. But in reality, their agenda has played out—and with the result that millions of people have either left the faith or never been brought up Catholic at all.

Many kinds of Catholics define themselves in opposition to Boomers along these lines. *They* are caught up in the worldly spirit of the age, while *we* are connected to the Holy Spirit through the inspiration of the Church throughout the ages. *They* have sacrificed the central gifts that the Church has to offer, while *we* are the guardians of these gifts. *Their* views are shallow, old, and tired, while *ours* have the depth and energy of true faith.

In a particularly mean remark, one that reeks of the kind of ageism that is totally inconsistent with loving someone as a brother in Christ, I've heard some wonder whether priests formed in this era fail to elevate the Host during the Liturgy of the Eucharist "because they don't believe in transubstantiation or because they are just too old to pull it off."

2. What Is in Our Hearts?

If you thought that last remark fails to respect the dignity of the human person and of fellow temples of the Holy Spirit, let me tell you that a quick search of anti—Vatican II memes online reveals that this is just the tip of the iceberg.

When this level of dismissiveness and mean-spiritedness comes out so powerfully, it outs those pedaling such junk as coming from a place other than the love Christ commanded us to have for one another. It is obviously not the kind of disagreement that comes from love, from genuine listening, or from a genuine encounter with the fullness of another person.

From where does it come?

It is worth focusing here on how often Jesus is concerned with what it is in the hearts of the Pharisees who are critiquing him (e.g., Mk 3, Lk 5). Indeed, sometimes—and maybe more often than we are prepared to admit—we are the ones being critiqued by Jesus via the Pharisees. Like them, we put limits on what God can do. Like them, we have a narrow-minded way of imagining how God is working in the world.

In the spirit of loving disagreement, and reserving the right to change our minds, we must examine our hearts and make sure that it is, in fact, the Holy Spirit who is guiding our critiques—and not the spirit of the Evil One who thrives on division and denigration.

One way I will try to do this is by telling a story or anecdote in each chapter that lifts up the dignity of the human person, resists the desire to define by opposition, and thickens out the reality of the very people who are being reduced to caricature. The one I've chosen here is quite personal.

3. A Story That Thickens

The only reason I'm a professor of Catholic moral theology— or, indeed, a practicing Catholic at all—is because of two spirit-of-Vatican-II Boomers: my mother and Fr. Steve Gibson.

Mom was raised Irish Catholic in deeply rural Ottawa, Illinois. (She met my father on a train going to see Notre Dame play Alabama in the 1973 Sugar Bowl.) Of course, she made sure all of us went to Sunday Mass: like clockwork at 6:15 p.m. on Sunday the Camosys were in the second or third pew just to the right of the altar at St. Mary's in Kenosha, Wisconsin. She also insisted that we get what she considered to be the right kind of post–Vatican II catechesis. She even pulled me out of a Catholic school I loved (boy could I still throw a mean tantrum at age twelve . . . sorry, Mom!) because I was getting a "pre–Vatican II" theological education there. And my siblings and I were much better off for changing schools.

In part because I showed interest in all things churchy (I would often walk to serve daily Mass at our local country church, even with only two or three people in the congregation), Mary Ann Camosy introduced me to scripture scholarship, ecclesiology, and the full range of our Church's moral teachings. Despite having always seen a deep connection between Mom's Catholicism and her support of the Democratic Party, when she heard I got my first job as communications director for Pro-Life Wisconsin, her eyes welled up with tears and she said, "I think Charlie is going to save a lot of babies."

The other is Fr. Steve Gibson, a priest ordained in the Congregation of Holy Cross (which founded the University of Notre Dame). He led retreats at Our Lady of Fatima Retreat Center on Notre Dame's campus that our family would attend annually. I can't say that the free football tickets weren't part of the reason we were there (I got spoiled during my formative years on late 1980s and early '90s Notre Dame football), but at least as important was the genuine spiritual renewal and nourishment we received—from Fr. Steve, the whole staff at the center, and fellow retreatants.

There was no "drawing God if God were a tree" here—there was prayer, singing (yes, accompanied by an acoustic guitar that Fr. Steve played), Mass (we were saying "and with your spirit" before it was cool), and many different kinds of activities (my parents probably didn't enjoy doing the "who gets the last seat in the lifeboat" ethics with a future moral theologian).

Oh, and there was something else. It was what I would later come to recognize as the spirit of Vatican II. People, lay-people, were *absolutely on fire*. I was one of them. My mom was another. So was a solid majority of everyone attending, in fact. I didn't recognize it as anything other than a place where the Holy Spirt was clearly on the move.

Only later, when I came to understand the divides in the Church, did I locate what I had experienced there in a particular "place" or "camp." Fr. Steve was doing what he was doing in part because he wanted people of the parish to choose him as their priest—something that he understood to be very much in the spirit of Vatican II, if not the letter. Indeed, he asked to be ordained a priest in 1970 in Uganda precisely because the local community there had asked for him to come. Now, Fr. Steve works in a very similar context at the Fr. Peyton Center in Ireland, named for the famous "Rosary priest" who was known for leading Rosary crusades in mammoth sports stadiums in the years prior to Vatican II.

Fr. Steve pointed out that several influential people at the Second Vatican Council used Fr. Peyton's model of the Rosary crusades to think about how the Church could adapt them to other areas. These crusades, in fact, started in the home, and then moved into the neighborhood, the parish, and then the diocese—empowering everyone along the way to be part of the eventual celebration for the thousands who would be there, not out of curiosity but because they had been part of it from the ground up.

4. What Are the Gifts and Truths Being Proclaimed?

Both my mother and Fr. Steve had a deep and profound experience that the Holy Spirit was moving the laity from the ground up as never before. Nothing about this experience of the faith, which I also shared, could be described as the watered-down, milquetoast, empty, culturally exhausted

Catholicism that defines the typical caricature. On the contrary, those of us who were lit on fire at this time were chomping at the bit to spread the Gospel to everyone.

And though I went through a dark time in my early twenties of questioning (and even probably something like agnosticism), being formed this way as a young person ensured that I would never totally let go of the faith. Indeed, it was the foundation that allowed me to come back even stronger when I made a full return to my faith in my late twenties.

Spirit-of-Vatican-II Boomers are "in their bones" Catholics who passed on a faith to me that is also now in my bones. By any reasonable measure, these fellow Catholics are vessels of the Holy Spirit, though the caricature of how they are thought of today often tries to hide or dismiss this fact.

The antagonistic binary of left versus right doesn't work here either. What are we to make of Fr. Steve, a spirit-of-Vatican-II priest who used the devotion of the Rosary to illustrate his vision of Church? What are we to make of a die-hard Democrat who was so proud of her son working for a pro-life organization that it brought her to tears?

Another gift of spirit-of-Vatican-II Catholics is that they lived through the times younger people today only talk about. They weren't LARPing (live-action role playing) or cosplaying the 1950s. They saw and experienced the changes in how Catholics practiced the faith from the 1960s through the 1980s and personally experienced the Holy Spirit work in their lives.

In many cases this generation—far from being content with smartphone slacktivism and political posturing around election time—actually went out into their communities and got their hands dirty serving their brothers and sisters. Peter Wolfgang, president of the pro-life Family Institute of Connecticut Action (certainly not someone who identifies with this approach!), recalled recently of the spirit-of-Vatican-II pastor in the parish where he grew up that "yes, we had the guitar and drums, altar boys in shorts and sneakers, a wreck-ovated interior, a congregation that stands after receiving Communion instead of kneeling, but then I opened the bulletin and read six pages of direct actions St. Bridget is taking on behalf of the poor that blows away any conservative parish I know."[1]

This generation also understands the legitimate diversity that can exist within the unity of the Church and how top-down power structures can sometimes stifle it. The liberating reforms of the Second Vatican Council, notes Notre Dame theologian John Cavadini, have produced beautifully inculturated liturgies across the world, especially in Africa. He attended a Mass celebrated according to the Rite of Zaire that "fully expressed the spirit of the liturgy of the universal Church not in spite of its being celebrated in an unmistakably African voicing, but *because* [emphasis added] of it."[2] He recounted that in a Mass he attended in Abuja; there was an eclectic mix of Gregorian chant, English hymnody, and local liturgical customs of the new priests' home villages, but his experience was one of the Holy Spirit "making the deepest possible appeal to our hearts."

Plus, this generation often does a better job of acknowledging that people are in different places in their journey toward the truth. Jesus spent his time with people who were far away from fully belonging to a community of faith. He said they needed a doctor of course, but he tended to them lovingly and included them in the community when others would not. Yes, he commanded them to go and sin no more, but he also said don't cast the first stone if you have sinned at all.

We need to balance the tension and include those who may be at various points in their journey, even those who seem to be quite far away. Indeed, Wolfgang notes that his "then pro-choice and happy atheist fiancée" may not have converted to Catholicism if it didn't come from the gentle invitation of a community led by spirit-of-Vatican-II Boomers.

5. What Are the Challenges?

So, yeah, here's the tough part, right? We want to fully acknowledge the gifts and the full, dignified humanity of a person or group—but then speak honestly in honoring the disagreement. Disagreement should be something we should work at achieving—something that takes place only after listening carefully and with humility.

Again, it should always be at the front of our minds that all other Catholics are our family members. And often a healthy family is one that can disagree fruitfully. The inclusion of multiple points of view can help a community incorporate ideas and information that otherwise might be missed. Therefore, those of us who aren't in this camp can and should try to be persuasive in the spirit of loving our brothers and sisters in Christ—and the Church we all call home.

Let's get the hard part out of the way first—like just ripping off the Band-Aid, right?

The simple fact of the matter is that the Church (at least in the rich, developed West) did very, very poorly when spirit-of-Vatican-II Catholics were the ones in charge. Parents and priests raised and shepherded young people who, over the last several decades, have overwhelmingly rejected the faith. Indeed, it is almost a cliché now to say that if ex-Catholics were a Christian denomination, they would be the largest one in the United States. And this problem, as we will see, is particularly acute with young people.

Now, some might say that this criticism isn't fair because disaffiliation with regard to religion has been ramping up across all Christian denominations in the West during this same period. But in his important book *Mass Exodus: Catholic Disaffiliation in Britain and America since Vatican*

II, Dr. Stephen Bullivant points out that it was in part a post-council watering down of the faith that got us into this mess.[3] Instead of inculturation, Catholics largely became assimilated into a larger culture that indeed was rejecting the faith. As Bullivant points out, we became like everybody else just as everybody else was starting to disaffiliate.

Indeed, those who have stayed in the Church are disproportionately those who identify themselves as more traditional. They tend to see the spirit of Vatican II as favoring the spirit of the current age over the gifts of the Church offered throughout the centuries. Instead of the banal liturgies that have come to dominate parishes after Vatican II, those who have stayed disproportionately crave a Mass in which we can perceive the Holy Spirit making the deepest possible appeal to their hearts. And they insist on a careful, robust, faithful catechesis in which the depth of the faith and the gifts of the Church's tradition are taught in ways that their truth and beauty shine for all to see and engage and live.

It is one thing for someone to reject the Catholic faith after they have understood what the Church teaches and why. But my experience with my students, and with folks on social media who are critical, is that they often have no idea what the actual teaching is—much less the reasoning behind the teaching.

Furthermore, while it is true that the Holy Spirit works from the ground up, unity in the Church cannot and does not come from a majority vote of the local people. When Archbishop Joseph Rummel excommunicated those in the Archdiocese of New Orleans who refused to integrate Catholic schools during the 1960s, he was standing up for a unifying truth in the Church: the dignity of the human person, especially as a bulwark against racism.[4] There are certain foundational teachings of the Church that may not be changed by a majority vote. Archbishop Rummel made the courageous choice to excommunicate those who so blatantly defied the teaching of Christ and his Church on the dignity of the human person.

There is room for very significant differences in the Church, and spirit-of-Vatican-II Catholics can help us see this. But the unity that flows from Baptism requires a common commitment to the central truths God has revealed and insisted be proclaimed and defended.

A final challenge is that we simply aren't in the era in which what the spirit-of-Vatican-II Boomers were up to is new and fresh and exciting. It has now been the way we've been doing things *for half a century.* There are new and fresh things coming into the Church from the ground up, especially from young laypeople today, but they are often pooh-poohed by older Catholics in this camp as "pre–Vatican II" or "trying to undo the council" or some such dismissive phrase.

6. Opportunities for Unity-in-Diversity

I suppose the central critique of spirit-of-Vatican-II Boomers is that invoking the "spirit of the council" in ways that can be interpreted so widely by so many people—with so many different and even contradictory ideas about the Church—makes the *unity* part of unity-in-diversity no longer clear. The result is it becomes unclear on what it means to be Catholic.

And with certain folks in this group, that may be a real impediment to actual dialogue. As I said from the beginning, what I'm proposing in this field guide won't work in every circumstance. But if we lead with what we are for (and not with what we are against), we set up the chance of finding common ground—of finding the least common denominator.

A good place to start is reflecting together on what the Second Vatican Council *actually said and did* through the texts of the official documents. For example:

- Was the call to return to the sources, and especially to scripture, much needed? (Absolutely.)
- Was it essential to focus on participation of the laity in the life of the Church and liturgy? (Um, yeah.)
- Was it important for the Church to acknowledge the truth in other religions and uphold religious freedom? (Outside of a few schismatic circles, it seems almost silly to imagine something different.)

Focusing on the texts as unifying not only creates the foundation for dialogue but also provides a bulwark against the spirit of Vatican II slipping into the spirit of the age. The texts say what they say—and don't say what they don't say.

And perhaps another area of common ground could be the *authority* of the documents of the council. We live in a remarkable age where a former papal representative to the United States let loose with both barrels, not just against the spirit of Vatican II but against the council itself.[5] Pope Francis, by contrast, insists that the authority of the council is final and even called it "irreversible."[6]

And what about authority more generally?

The papacy of Pope Francis has been met with significant dissent from areas of the Church I would never have expected. We see challenges to Church teaching about liturgy and religious freedom, yes, but also the right to migrate, the universal destination of goods, and the death penalty. The authority of the Church's teaching, especially as it unites the Body of Christ in a shared understanding of the dignity of the human person proclaimed by the Gospel, could maybe somewhat paradoxically be an important tool of dialogue with many spirit-of-Vatican-II Boomers.

The genuinely good, important stuff above is, I believe, low-hanging fruit. But if we can be strong enough to persist in our commitment to dialogue—if all those involved can embrace "Jesus forsaken" and stay with our family members over some extended time—even more would become available to us.

Think for a moment about the implications of authority and unity in the Church. If it is necessary for us to be unified about the texts of Vatican II and modern Catholic social teaching (beginning with *Rerum Novarum*), is it insane to think we couldn't extend the conversation to other areas? Even to, oh, I don't know, what Canon 212 says about correcting bishops?

Now, before you try to have me committed, consider what Canon 212 actually says: yes, faithful Catholics are "bound to follow with Christian obedience" those who have authority in the Church in balanced tension, but *also* laypeople with the proper knowledge and competence "have the right and even at times *the duty*" (my emphasis) to let their opinions be known to those who have authority in the Church.

Is it outrageous to think that, over time, there could be a unifying dialogue about—as recent chancellor of the Diocese of Dallas Gregory Caridi put it—"How to Correct Bishops Correctly"?[7] There's so much common ground to be had if we just stay in contact with each other consistently. How about a quick list of other points of agreement to think about?

- *A focus on the Catholic laity (and skepticism of clericalism) in the fullness of our diversity.* This would include everything from Opus Dei to the *National Catholic Reporter*.

- *A genuinely consistent life ethic.* This is one that acknowledges the horrific practices and numbers when it comes to abortion but focuses on a broad array of social justice issues as well—including supporting women and families at risk for abortion.

- *A healthy skepticism of technology.* This is especially important to our generation, which has seen what it has done to the culture.

- *A resistance to those false social justice movements.* By this I mean those that reduce the human person merely to the structures and systems in which they live.

Finally, let's acknowledge something that is absolutely essential in the mix here: the idea that there is something called the Holy Spirit mysteriously and supernaturally at work in the world defies our cultural slouch toward the view that everything can be ultimately reduced to matter in motion. Many spirit-of-Vatican-II folks, it turns out, wholeheartedly believe in a spiritual reality, the infusion of nature with God's divine grace, and the Church as a vehicle for God's saving grace in the world. Many believe this in their very bones, in the deepest part of who they are, and simply cannot imagine their life without any other assumption. This is common ground for everyone—including more traditional Catholic young people—looking around for anyone who will take the reality of the spiritual realm seriously.

Conclusion

Getting to a place where we can find unity-in-diversity will take time and commitment. It will take intentionally avoiding all kinds of political idolatry and defining ourselves by opposition to our perceived opponents. And, let's face it, on whichever side of a dialogue we are, this kind of thing is going to provide many opportunities for us to choose to be the first to love, listen with humility, and unite to the sufferings of Jesus forsaken.

But there is also a reason to think about these kinds of relationships as adventures. Who are we to limit the way God may use our willingness to dialogue with a spirit-of-Vatican-II Boomer?

So, *let's go*! Visit that parish guitar Mass you dislike so intensely, the one your neighbor goes to, and invite her to coffee afterward. We have work to do! Or, better, God does.

Oh, and speaking of trads . . .

3

The Trad Millennial

I.e., "The Guardian of Tradition Catholic"

1. The Thin Caricature

You've heard of bingo memes? Some (usually funny) person puts together a virtual bingo card with squares that are meant to make a witty and sometimes biting point about a person or group. For instance, when I just googled "Chicago Cubs bingo card" I found an older meme with squares making derogatory comments in jest about how the players look or perform, like "Arrieta's Beard Looks Especially Intimating" and "Marte Makes Unnecessary Diving Catch."

These memes are a wonderful example of what this book is trying to cultivate. Yes, in a certain sense that meme was making fun of Cubs players, but it was made by and for the Cubs' family. It was put together out of the kind of familial love that permits this kind of poking fun.

One can find hundreds of these bingo memes online—including those that, you guessed it, poke fun at young traditional Catholics. Here are some of what I consider the best examples of the bingo squares, which are good ways of beginning to think about the thin caricature of this group:

- "Babies Who Die before Baptism Get Limbo at Best"
- "The USCCB Is Communist"

- Complains about Women Wearing Pants
- "Error Has No Rights!"
- Pretends to Speak French or Italian for Some Reason
- "Actually, the Inquisitors Did Nothing Wrong"
- Weirdly into Christopher Columbus
- "The Latin Mass Is for All Time!"

I mention "young" traditional Catholics (or "trads") above, but I think it is important to note that Millennials are now in their forties! (As a Gen-Xer this is kind of shocking for me to write—as it makes me *even older*.) So, while we may think of these trads as young, many are not *that* young. Many have kids. Many have *lots* of kids.

Some of you may recognize the thin caricature above, yes? Among other things, there is a sense that this group is obsessed with rules simply for the sake of rules, ignores or even criticizes the social teachings of the Church (even when proclaimed by the US bishops), rejects democratic values like the right to freedom of speech and freedom of religion, tries to defend even the most indefensible parts of the Church's history (especially as part of a monolithic view of the Christian tradition), and—the traditional Latin Mass.

Oh *boy*, the Latin Mass.

Often the critique of younger trads fits very nicely into the liberal/conservative Roman Catholicism binary fight to the death that this book is at pains to avoid—think *Commonweal* and the *National Catholic Reporter* on the left versus "the trads" on the right. Here, for instance, is Church historian Massimo Faggioli writing in *Commonweal*:

> Those who have contact with young Catholics—for example, college students—may have noticed that this theological anti-liberalism is not just coming from a few marginal intellectuals. . . . It may be

expressed as an enthusiasm for the Tridentine Mass and a distaste for the Novus ordo. Or it may take the form of an interest in countercultural communities—in some version of the "Benedict Option." But it can also take the form of a theo-political imagination that rejects liberal democracy in favor of a new Christendom. Mixed in with this ideal is often a suspicion of those who come from parts of the world where Christianity is not the predominant religion.[1]

Or how about Michael Sean Winters, author of *God's Right Hand: How Jerry Falwell Made God a Republican and Baptized the American Right*, critiquing trads who were disappointed in Pope Francis's ruling against the Latin Mass in the *National Catholic Reporter*: "Seminarians who are asking older priests to teach them how to say the old rite need to be more focused on improving their bedside manner for hospital visits."[2] In this view, traditional Catholics not only reject democratic values but also want to retreat into a Benedict Option–style countercultural community and prepare to create a racist Christian Empire in which everyone goes to Latin Mass instead of caring for the vulnerable sick.

2. What Is in Our Hearts?

Man, that last critique was harsh.

Like each of the groups we're examining, trad Millennials face their share of challenges, no doubt about it. But what's going on in the hearts of those who make this kind of thin and flat caricature of these Catholics?

Some who identify with "the left" side of the incoherent-and-destructive-binary-fight-to-the-death in US Catholicism often imagine themselves as the ones who are open-minded, liberating, and fighting for legitimate diversity within the Church. But the dismissive and even cruel caricature described above is, well, working directly against every one of those values.

Recall from the previous chapter that *we* are often the ones Jesus is critiquing when he hammers the Pharisees. *We* are the ones who are putting limits on what God can do. *We* are the ones with the narrow-minded way of imagining that God is working in the world.

Sure, there are legitimate criticisms to make, and we will make them below. But making them in an authentic way requires that we search our own hearts as to whether something else is playing a role here as well. Just as some let their disdain for "guitar Masses" get in the way of seeing how God is working in his Church, disdain for the whole trad energy, style, and "vibe" can also blind us to the Holy Spirit at work.

3. A Story That Thickens

Very often, being forced to chew on the story of a real person can force us out of our antagonistic comfort zones. Well, good readers, chew on this one.

Steve Adubato is a trad Millennial. One who writes for *both* the *National Catholic Reporter* and *Catholic World Report*. His *Patheos* blog will hammer "purity culture" one week and discuss the care with which he teaches St. John Paul II's Theology of the Body the next.[3]

And where was he doing this teaching? At St. Benedict's Preparatory School in Newark, New Jersey, serving mostly at-risk people of color.[4] Full disclosure: Steve was an undergraduate student of mine at Fordham University in New York City, but that he was formed in such a progressive context makes his story even more layered and complex. A self-described "weird Catholic," Steve argues that his traditional Catholicism is an "impetus to engage more deeply with the sounds and needs of today's world."[5]

You may wonder: what is the liturgical preference for this young man so concerned for social justice?

The Latin Mass, of course. He "fell in love with its richness" and saw it as a bulwark against watered-down Christianity with a "drab liturgy" and homilies that boiled down to "Jesus wants you to be nice to people." Steve, especially as a young person, was more attracted to Catholics like Dorothy Day who connected traditional doctrine and liturgy with concern for those on the margins.

And are you ready for this? As a trad Millennial, Steve has had a particular focus on what it is like to be a queer Catholic and says that he's inspired by thinkers and activists like the lesbian Catholic Eve Tushnet who describes chastity and celibacy "not as obstacles to intimacy, but as entry ways into a deeper mode of living in relationship with others." He also shares Tushnet's experience of responding more strongly to older forms of liturgy and spirituality that tend to place greater emphasis on beauty, the body, and the material realm as a whole.

Steve even argues that it is Pope Benedict XVI, not Pope Francis, who is the real "gay icon," given his "flair for the gothic and grandiose," his "appreciation for aesthetic beauty and the arts," and his "taste for extravagant liturgical vestments and pageantry!"

But Steve is no hater of Pope Francis. Rather, he urges trads to "rely on Francis' image of the Church as a field hospital and enter into the world with our alternative vision."

4. What Are the Gifts and Truths Being Proclaimed?

The message of many Millennial trads is twofold: (1) something was lost after Vatican II related to the beauty of the traditions of the Church, and (2) many younger people are rediscovering that tradition in ways that defy what have been more typical right/left disputes within the Church.

Rachel Lu, a Catholic convert and philosophy professor at St. Thomas University in Minnesota, writing in *America* magazine, captures this sense well:

> My traditionalist friends opened doors to verdant pastures that I had never seen. We prayed rosaries and novenas, watched "Life Is Worth Living," and got together on the feast of St. Edmund Campion for a dramatic reading of "Campion's Brag." There were lively arguments about the merits of Pius IX's Syllabus of Errors and whether it would be pleasant to live in Franco's Spain. Some of it was absurd, some uplifting, but I was fascinated by the way traditionalists seemed to live on the plane of the entire Catholic tradition. Saints and heroes sprang from the grass for them. The Battle of Lepanto was as real in their minds as the ongoing war in Iraq.[6]

Some of what is going on here is that the kinds of traditional liturgies and practices these (mostly) young people are embracing are highly resistant to the "hey, it's just me and my smartphone" techno-individualist culture they are trying to avoid in their quest for spiritual growth.

Notre Dame professor of liturgy Kimberly Belcher studied students at three Midwest Catholic campuses and found that practices such as eucharistic adoration are effective at helping them resist the particular stresses on college students today.[7] Adoration is a time and space when they will not be interrupted by the highs generated by dopamine hits from likes and comments on their latest carefully cultivated photo and the lows of FOMO coming from looking at hundreds of other carefully cultivated photos. It is a space of authentic beauty and rest with deeply moving reminders of the presence, majesty, and providence of God and the chance to stop and reset one's life in light of those realities.

And here's a very important part of the trad movement among younger people: in an atomized, individualist world (again, especially as it exists in social media), these traditional liturgical and devotional practices give young people a real, embodied sense of community and belonging.

Indeed, many of these things put together make for an extremely dedicated community of faith. Before he served the Diocese of San Angelo, Texas, Bishop Michael James Sis served in campus ministry at Texas A&M and instituted eucharistic adoration at the request of his students. He had to cut off devotion during overnight hours so that his students could get some sleep. When the 2021 controversy over the Latin Mass was in full swing, an old friend of mine from high school wrote me to say that his nineteen-year-old son loves the Latin Mass so much that he was planning to bring a car to college so he can go to it in the only place it existed in his area, a town several miles away from campus.

In a world in which it can be difficult to motivate teenage and twentysomething young men to engage much of anything outside of video games and porn, this kind of dedication is impressively countercultural.

So, yes, young trads have plenty of gifts to offer the Church. They remind us all of the power of tradition and ritual; of the responsibility we have to pass on our faith; of the need for a sense of God's mystery, power, and transcendence; of the reality of objective truth and the power of art, beauty, and the body; and of the ability of all of this to produce highly motivated communities of people—and not just individuals—who are growing in faith.

And let me blow your mind with this final thought: young trads also show us a central truth present in both the spirit and letter of—wait for it—*Vatican II*. Namely, the importance of an energized and dynamic laity who are willing to assert themselves in asking the hierarchical Church for what they need in order to be spiritually fed. These are some of the most active laypeople in the life of the Church today—with full, conscious, and active participation in their liturgical practices. In fact, a case can be made that this kind of participation is stronger in a Latin Mass than in the average Mass most Catholics attend on Sundays.

5. What Are the Challenges?

Rachel Lu, despite helping us understand the gifts that trads bring to the table, doesn't shy away from the challenges of this group either. She found that people in her new community could be "prickly, arrogant, and stubborn." She had more than her share of encounters with what she calls "reactionaries and oddballs." As part of her introduction to this community, she has met everyone from Young Earth creationists to 9/11 truthers.

And she has also known some people who were "tempted by schism."

There is lots of pain associated with Vatican II in the trad Catholic community—especially among the older crowd that had seen much of the beauty, tradition, and meaning in the Church they loved unilaterally taken away from them. And from a younger crowd that, again, felt as if they'd been denied much of their Catholic inheritance. But the temptation of formal rupture with the Body of the Christ is real and can be a major challenge for some within trad circles, just as a judgmental spirit can be toward all those other Catholics.

These issues may arise from the deeply problematic desire to put limits on God that is shared by many groups, for instance, to keep God in a place where one is comfortable: the tabernacle, the Latin Mass, and the pre–Vatican II Church.

On one level, of course, something about this instinct is correct. God is obviously not in every half-baked idea offered on TikTok or whatever social theory is being pushed by academics at the moment. Yet, sinfulness and self-deception are central human realities that should temper our enthusiasm when it comes assuming new things are of God.

But on another level, it is also true that the Spirit does in fact blow where it will and God's ways are not our ways. If we truly believe that God's grace is working through the Catholic Church, we must at times put aside our limited human understanding and personal preferences and pay attention to the new things God is doing, even when they seem counterintuitive and push us in directions we weren't expecting. Sinfulness and self-deception can also keep us from seeing that God is doing something new.

When we put God into a box—and decide where God can go and what God can or cannot do—this is a form of idolatry. And the result of this kind of idolatry in many trad communities is not pretty. They involve things like disparagement of the current Novus Ordo liturgy, glowing rhetoric about schismatics like Archbishop Marcel Lefebvre, and a straight-up-no-chaser rejection of Vatican II in its entirety.

In short: it is a rejection of the Catholic Church as it exists today in favor of the "true Church"—which, as it turns out, is their very different Church.

To be clear, this is not coming from just a few cranks with a screw loose. Recently, Michael Brendan Dougherty of *National Review* wrote an op-ed in the *New York Times* defending raising his family in a traditional Latin Mass community. But this author and public figure (one whom I respect deeply on other matters) went on to claim that the "new Mass" is *not part of the same religion* in which his children have been raised.[8]

This is the kind of statement that prompted Pope Francis to address with *Traditionis Custodes*, a document that attempted to focus on the unity of the Church—a unity that reaffirms the authority of Vatican II and post-conciliar popes in ways that tries to keep the Church together. Whether we attend the "new Mass," the Tridentine Latin Mass, or Divine Liturgy in an Eastern Catholic Church (no one remembers they exist!), we are all part of the same religion.

6. Opportunities for Unity-in-Diversity

Irony alert: those who find Pope Francis's moves in this direction problematic (and even painful) are in much the same place that spirit-of-Vatican-II Catholics have found themselves for decades: longing for a Church that is quite different from the one that currently exists. A commitment to unity-in-diversity means swallowing a painful pill, checking our pride, following the Holy Spirit's lead in our own lives, and trusting that Christ and his Church are bigger than all of this.

Mount Mercy University professor Taylor Patrick O'Neill put it well on social media: "It is indeed possible to be personally upset or worried about *Traditionis Custodes* and to continue to love Pope Francis, to pray for him, and to give him all due obedience and deference as the Supreme Pontiff and Vicar of Christ. In fact, it is required."

And there is also no reason at all why the unity that comes from obedience and deference cannot also be made to work within a Church that makes room for legitimate diversity within its liturgies.

In the previous chapter we saw John Cavadini highlight the incredible liturgical diversity that exists within global Catholicism. The liturgy can and does shift to meet the needs of the local people. The liturgy can and does shift to address new insights gained by the Church over time. (Most trads will agree, for instance, it was good to take out the Good Friday Prayer that invoked "the perfidious Jews.") So, yes, the "new Mass" is an innovation, but so was the Latin Mass that came into being more than 600 years after Christ. That's as far removed from the day of Christ as our day is removed from the Middle Ages.

Again, if we really think that the Holy Spirit is working through the Church, then who are we to put limits on what God is doing? Or the space God is making to reach his people through the liturgy?

And that works for "the left" as much as "the right."

Could those who strongly support Pope Francis's central concern in *Traditionis Custodes* nevertheless make space for what God is clearly doing via the Latin Mass and more traditional practices? Refusing to put limits on God in this way is on the side of inclusivity and legitimate diversity within the Catholic family.

This is not just an invitation to a straight and able-bodied majority, either. As previously cited, the Latin Mass is an important liturgical home for many same-sex-attracted Catholics. And it turns out that it is also very important for many Catholics with one or more disabilities.

For instance, as Steve Adubato reminds us, a good number of Catholics on the autism spectrum attend traditional Latin Masses because of the sense of structure and safety it provides.[9] Many blind and deaf Catholics also appear to prefer the Latin Mass.[10] Furthermore, the Latin Mass can serve as a place of refuge for sex abuse victims who suffered in the context of the post–Vatican II Church.

Rightly understood (that is, in the context of deference to the unifying authority of Vatican II and of the Holy Father), the Extraordinary Form of the Mass and other traditional liturgical practices can be wonderful examples of legitimate catholic-with-a-small-c diversity. Sure, some misapplications take place—but why focus on these and ignore those that occur in the Ordinary form of the liturgy? Pope Francis is right to think of the Church as a field hospital for those on the peripheries, but those who inhabit these spaces may not fit our preconceived ideas about who they are.

A commitment to unity-in-diversity means finding a way to make room for those who love the Latin Mass. Many also subscribe and assent to the unifying authority of Vatican II and consider Pope Francis and his predecessors fully legitimate authorities. There is no reason to throw the baby out with the schismatic bathwater. Perhaps today's Latin Mass communities need to be disciplined in some ways or more fully integrated into the larger parish communities in which they exist. Perhaps more emphasis could be placed on communities that would prefer the current rite to be offered *ad orientem* (that is, with the priest leading the congregation in prayer by facing the same direction they are). Many Catholics of all stripes are open to the use of at least some Latin at Mass.

These kinds of moves will not satisfy everyone, of course. But that's what it means to be part of a universal Church—a universal, Catholic family—that tries to balance unity and diversity. When *Traditionis Custodes* was first released, my friend Jeff Morrow, professor of theology at Seton Hall University, offered some important words on social media to put the frustrations many were feeling into context:

> The Catholic Church, for everything that it is, is also a very large family. It is clearly more than that, but it also is that. I have seven children, which no longer seems to me to be very large, but what living as a father and husband in a family of nine people has taught me is that not everyone always understands or agrees with decisions that are being made. Recently (as in a few weeks ago) our family moved to a new home in a new town. That was a decision my wife and I made for the good of our family. Was it the right decision to make? I don't have absolute certitude that it was. But, as the parents of our family, we have the authority to make such decisions, even when it upsets some of our children. One child

> in particular has made comments like, "But it's not the best decision for me. You never make the best decision for me." This child might be correct, at least with the first part of that comment (the child might also be incorrect . . . time might tell). But as parents of more than one child, we can't always make decisions that affect the entire family based on one child's needs. We have to make the best decisions we can for the good of the whole family.

My friend Jeff said this in the context of his children rebelling—and doing so in ways that, while regrettable, he nevertheless found understandable. This is a story that is instructive for the family of the Church—on multiple levels.

For those who bear the burden of authority, Jeff's story demonstrates the need to allow one's children to rebel and offer their reasons for why they disagree. But the story is also instructive for those of us who are bound by this authority. It means that, at times, decisions will be made by our leaders that, while not in our personal best interest, are nevertheless in the best interests of the family as a whole.

Conclusion

In a Church like ours, it just isn't possible for the authorities to act in such a way that reflects the best interests of every single individual member of the Catholic family. But it doesn't follow from this that we can't do better than we are right now. We can and should do better. Indeed, we must do better.

In thinking about how to envision what this might look like, I'm drawn back to "the two Steves." Fr. Steve Gibson, discussed at some length in chapter 2, was a mentor of mine. The other, Steve Adubato, profiled in this chapter, was a student of mine. Both Steves are located in very different places within the Church: culturally, theologically, liturgically, demographically, and more.

And *yet*.

Despite them being quite different from each other, these two Steves are nevertheless very much bound up together through the unity of the Church. Steve Adubato, though very much a trad Millennial, doesn't limit God to the tabernacle of the Latin Mass. Steve Gibson, though very much a spirit-of-Vatican-II Boomer, has focused much of his life on devotion to the Rosary. Both are committed to more contemporary trends in social justice, and both are committed to honoring the Church's centuries-old traditions.

This is what unity-in-diversity could look like and what the Church could and should strive for.

4

The Gen Z "None"

I.e., "The Homeless Seeker"

1. The Thin Caricature

A headline from satirical "news" website *The Onion* read: "Brain-Dead Teen, Only Capable of Rolling Eyes and Texting, to Be Euthanized."[1]

The image that went with the story was both funny and priceless: a teen girl on her bed, staring vacantly at her phone as if she were somehow both annoyed and bored with life itself and clearly couldn't be bothered with anything that wasn't on the glowing rectangle in front of her face.

This is the kind of image, I suspect, that comes to mind for many of us when we think of a Gen Z "None." A young person with their smartphone glued to their hand—too lazy and/or addicted to care much about anything besides who liked which photos on Instagram or thinking about how to go viral on TikTok. Some are obsessed with curating social status on their "Insta" while offering their unpopular opinions on their "Finsta," the name for their fake/private account. Others spend most of their time playing video games and watching porn—developing the kind of habits and academic record that will make it difficult for them to succeed or even become interested in college.

The "none" in the title of this chapter refers to this generation's relationship with organized religion. The rise of those who will claim "none" when it comes to religious affiliation, particularly among Generation Z (which at the time I write consists of preteens through young adults in their mid- to late twenties), has been documented for some time now. Younger people are significantly less likely to identify with organized religion than those who are older.[2]

But let's continue with the caricature. If this generation has the remnants of something like passionate religious belief, they have replaced it with a kind of hyper-online wokeism (a particularly strident leftist social justice vision focused on race, sex/gender, and sexual orientation). Many move from fake outrage to fake outrage directed against an *out-group* but expressed to signal their virtue in order to gain credibility with (or avoid being "canceled" by) their preferred *in-group*.

Furthermore, because they have been mostly shielded from bad things happening to them via overprotective "helicopter" parents, Gen Z is so emotionally fragile that they are largely unable to thoughtfully encounter people with views other than their own. They instead respond as so-called snowflakes who, if not affirmed in everything important to them, get "triggered" and are unable to cope with their emotions enough to engage in a rational discussion.

All of this (along with, again, a general sense that they can't be bothered to do anything that doesn't involve a smartphone) has led to the presumption that Gen Z is made up largely of agnostics and atheists, that they either don't care about religion or are actively hostile to it.

2. What Is in Our Hearts?

As with all the caricatures we are critically examining in this book, there are some difficult truths present in the false picture being painted. To distinguish between what's true and what's false, it will once again be important to get ourselves into the quiet and prayerful place where we can honestly and forthrightly reflect on our own biases and blind spots.

It can be difficult to ask the "Are *we* the baddies?" question. Let us once again recall that we are often the ones Jesus is critiquing when he hammers the Pharisees. But sometimes we are the ones who are putting limits on what God can do. We are the ones with the narrow-minded way of imagining how God is working in the world.

Could that be true of the way we think about Gen Z? Is it possible that, especially for us older folks, we are tempted toward the kind of "get off my lawn!" reactions that don't give this group a fair shot?

Gen Z is the first generation to grow up with smartphones and social media around as a matter of course. For those of us who didn't grow up this way, it can be difficult to access a world so intimately connected to these technologies and platforms. But, especially for those of us who are Gen X, I imagine our parents thought something similar about how much time we spent talking on the phone, watching TV, or playing Nintendo, right? And did we turn out that bad?

Before you other generations answer that, maybe we can admit that understanding across generations has almost always proven difficult. It's something close to a cliché to comment about how the World War II generation brought with them life experiences and assumptions that made it difficult for them to understand the "sex, drugs, and rock and roll" culture of their children, the Baby Boomers.

So, let's start there. If we are older, we are already at a disadvantage given the generational differences in play.

But let's push further. Gen Z does tend to have very strong views about race, sex/gender, and sexual orientation. They may not be correct in holding all of them, but could part of our reaction be based in part on such an instinctual and powerful distaste for these views such that we simply dismiss them in one fell swoop? If we can just dismiss most of a generation as "woke snowflakes"—without wrestling and contending with some of the things this generation gets right—then perhaps *we* are the real snowflakes.

This is especially true if we take seriously the Church's teaching on matters of social justice. Very often, and I say this with the authority of someone who is a teacher of this generation, Gen Z simply doesn't know anything about the documents and work of Catholic social teaching. Indeed, the kind of watered-down "Christian" faith they have been exposed to, and even taught by older generations, might be described as something like "Moral Therapeutic Deism."[3] This is the view that God is largely not involved in the world but wants us to be nice and affirm others so that we can all achieve the central goal of life, which can be defined succinctly as "feeling good about ourselves."

If this is the view of faith they have encountered, is it any wonder that Gen Z disproportionately answers "none" on surveys asking about religious affiliation? Who would want to be part of such a painfully boring and inconsequential faith? I know I wouldn't want any part of it.

Happily, and contrary to the caricature above, many "Zoomers" (as they are sometimes called) are seeking out a more substantial and fruitful spiritual path. And the story in the next section is of someone who exemplifies this tendency.

3. A Story That Thickens

This is a story about a young Black woman named Chloé Valdary. She's on the older end of Gen Z, but she reveals so much that is important about this generation. This tweet from her, all by itself, reveals so much:

> If you wanted to know how my quarantine has been going, in addition to my startup, I've been

> meditating for an hour a day and studying Jordan
> Peterson and Abraham Lincoln and Toni Morrison
> and Christianity and Dr. King and Buddhism.[4]

It is astonishing how much this single tweet reveals about this young woman and her generation:

- She worked on a startup during the pandemic.

- She meditates for an hour a day.

- She's reading about Martin Luther King Jr., Abraham Lincoln, and Jordan Peterson at the same time.

- She finds truth and wisdom in both Christianity and Buddhism.

The backstory of this tweet is that Valdary was well on her way to becoming something like the caricature discussed above when she had a transformative experience with her agnostic religious studies professor.[5]

This professor had shown them a documentary titled *Jesus Camp*, which followed a group of evangelicals at their summer camp for kids. In the face of a student railing against these Christians, the professor surprised Valdary by vigorously defending them, explaining that they, like all people, gravitate toward things that give them meaning, significance, belonging, and community.

And the professor, now engaged in a shouting match with the student, exclaimed: "If you dehumanize people who have different beliefs than you do, you are completely missing the point of this class!"

It was during her college years when Valdary said she started "outgrowing my religion" and decided to move into activism. And it was this activism that led to her starting up a conflict resolution program she called "Theory of Enchantment," something she described as "growing my religion." She was reacting against a culture that she describes as "alienated, atomized, hyper mechanical, bureaucratic, and disenchanted."[6] Using both pop culture and texts by important thinkers, she created a conflict resolution program rooted in three fundamentals:

- Treat people like human beings, not political abstractions.
- Criticize to uplift and empower, never to tear down, never to destroy.
- Root everything you do in love and compassion.

Though she has moved away from the Christian religion in which she was raised, it is clear that Valdary—like many young people who have made similar moves—never quite quit "religion" entirely and still finds it quite necessary. In fact, she still describes Christianity as "one of the most successful memes of all time."[7]

So many young "nones" find themselves in a space much like hers. But what do they have to do with unity in the Church when they don't identify themselves as Catholic? Consider Sam, who says he is Catholic in some sense but that it only "partly defines him" and "doesn't limit him." In a recent *National Catholic Reporter* article, he further explained:

> I discovered a lot of other kinds of inner spiritual traditions. I like to say, when you're finding God in silence, it doesn't really matter what you call God: It's the same God. The Sufi tradition in Islam, I find, resonates with my experiences. Also, the contemplative tradition and different Indian practices of nonduality and mindfulness, Buddhism, all these things.[8]

No doubt many Muslims and Buddhists would find themselves more than slightly annoyed with Sam claiming that they worship the "same" deity as the Triune God of the Christian tradition, but, again, let's leave these mistakes aside. Instead, let's focus on this important fact: the loss of faith in particular religious institutions has not kept Gen Z from having religious interests and beliefs. The research bears this out.

While they are the most diverse and complex US generation that has ever existed, including when it comes to their faith, the Springtide Research Institute nevertheless found that "78 percent of people ages 13–25 consider themselves at least slightly spiritual, including 60 percent of unaffiliated young people (atheists, agnostics and nones). And 71 percent say they are at least slightly religious, including 38 percent of the unaffiliated."[9] Indeed, they found that "60 percent of teens and young adults who are not involved with an organized religion described themselves as spiritual, and 19 percent said they attend religious gatherings at least once a month."[10] Yes, they often have an "unbundled" religious sensibility—but when it comes to those with a Catholic background, a greater proportion of Gen Z Catholics have become more religious (37 percent) than less religious (24 percent) in the past five years. Furthermore, more young Catholics have grown in their faith during the pandemic (38 percent) than those who have doubted more (13 percent) or lost their faith completely (7 percent). Nearly seven in ten young Catholics (68 percent) say that religion shapes their daily life, and a whopping 91 percent consider themselves to be at least slightly religious.[11]

4. What Are the Gifts and Truths Being Proclaimed?

Both the story of Chloé Valdary specifically and the research on Gen Z generally blow up the caricature with which we began. This isn't a generation in danger of becoming agnostic or irreligious. But they do have important critiques to make about our institutions, including our (Catholic) religious institutions.

Think about this: given that the stories of the sex abuse crisis broke in the United States in 2002, this generation has never known a Catholic Church apart from that very public crisis. Especially with the clericalism, intrigue, abuse of power, and guilt at the highest levels (see the case of Cardinal Theodore McCarrick's abuse and cover-up as a classic example), surely we can understand why this generation is largely skeptical of the institutional Church. Again, this comes not from a particular animus for religion or faith but from Gen Z being skeptical of all large, slow-moving institutions that lack transparency and abuse power.

And this reaction isn't just based on the injustices and abuses involved. It is also based on their own experiences of these institutions. Their addiction to smartphones (and social media), exacerbated by the challenges of the pandemic, has turned this into the loneliest generation of young people in history. The Springtide report found that 45 percent of young Catholics feel that no one understands them, while an astonishing 65 percent have three or fewer meaningful interactions in a regular day.

And if that weren't heart-wrenching enough, only 1 percent—*1 percent!*—said that a religious leader checked in on them as the pandemic-related lockdowns and distancing began in spring 2020.

Gen Z has rightly called out many Catholic institutions for failing to be the home of authentic communities that serve the real needs of real people—again, not because they have a particular animus for religious institutions but because *they desperately need and want this kind of community*. Springtide found that relationships are far more important than the actual teachings of the Church on particular issues. Gen Z wants relationships. They want to be listened to. They want a consistent presence they can trust. Indeed, the presence of even *one* trusted adult within an organization made them feel they belong. But many don't have even that.

And those of us who take the time to listen might be surprised with what we will find. This is not some snowflake generation incapable of having discussions about differences. Springtide found that 68 percent would not stop speaking to someone who strongly disagreed or opposed their political values and 77 percent want to have conversations about differences openly. A full 81 percent of young people said it is important to try to understand both sides of a political issue, and 84 percent agree that getting educated about the views and perspectives of others is important for seeing the different sides more clearly.

Perhaps the rest of us can return the favor? Sure, these young people may get some things wrong about what radical love and acceptance *mean*—but young people who aggressively defend and promote radical love and acceptance already have the instinct and foundation of a Christian love.

All of this, coupled with a strong desire for enchantment and religious belief, should give us all quite a bit of hope for Gen Z!

5. What Are the Challenges?

We are now in the right frame of mind to turn to some of the genuine challenges faced by this generation.

First, and perhaps most important, there is no such thing as the Roman Catholic Church without the authority of the institution. We've seen the debate over how, precisely, the authority of the institution functions in various ways—especially for spirit-of-Vatican-II Boomers and trad Millennials. But with Gen Z "nones," the challenge is even more profound: the institution itself seems up for grabs.

And this has some predictable results. Young people like Sam who collapse all religious traditions into "the same God" simply do not take, say, the grounding authority of the Nicene Creed on God's Triune nature seriously and are thus

completely adrift in their religious journey. The authority of
the Church, in protecting and teaching the truths of God's
divine revelation, provides the foundation for not only one's
beliefs about God but also one's moral vision. The individual
dignity of the human person, which underlies our duty of
radical love and acceptance, is grounded in a particular vision
of the good. Contrary to what Sam would have us believe, it
is *not* the same as a Buddhist vision that denies the idea of
individuality as an illusion that produces suffering.

A healthy skepticism for big institutions must be balanced
by a commitment to certain foundational truths that cannot
be watered down or dismissed with a "meh, isn't it really all
just the same thing at the end of the day?" Irony alert: the
very justice-centered impulses that are so impressive in this
generation require them to abandon their swishy appeals to
"Who am I to judge?" relativism.

To be a Catholic Christian advocating for radical love and
acceptance—especially for the least among us on the margins
of the culture—requires a strong defense of certain objective
truths about the human person. And given that this defense
needs to be made over centuries in multiple cultural contexts
(some of which are hostile), an authoritative institution is
absolutely necessary in order to preserve this vision.

Again, we've seen that there is a balance to be maintained
between an individual Catholic's freedom of conscience and
the obedience that is due to the institutional Church. But Gen
Z thinks that identities are infinitely malleable and that they
can be formed and built from an endless list of sources that
the individual autonomously chooses. As a result, they put
themselves outside a Church that insists we have been given
an unchangeable identity from God, from his Church, and
from our families.

Despite the lie told to young people at every turn that this
is oppressive and stifling, it is actually a liberating freedom to

know that much about our identity is unchosen and beyond our control.

Indeed, the constant pressure to choose from a near-infinite number of identities—especially in the context of having to perform them on multiple social media platforms—has produced horrific results for Gen Z. It isn't just the profound loneliness that comes from having so few authentic and meaningful interactions but also the dramatically increased rates of anxiety, depression, and even suicide that come from becoming so alienated from our given identity when we don't have a sense of who we are apart from social media performances.

6. Opportunities for Unity-in-Diversity

"It's not one thing, it's multiple things."

This is how Chloé Valdary described how she is "growing her religion" via the Theory of Enchantment.[12] And on the one hand, this is at the heart of what it means to be Catholic—what it means to be part of a universal Church. We can and have borrowed, adapted, and been challenged by an astonishing range of cultural influences, philosophical ideas, and theological visions over two millennia.

And to the extent that Gen Z's impulse is to live the life of a seeker who mines these traditions of light and wisdom that give us new insight into our faith, they can be right at home in the Catholic Church. My best friend in graduate school at Notre Dame was a former Buddhist converted to an utterly orthodox and devout Catholic. But he also never lost many of the central insights he gained as a Buddhist, including a healthy skepticism of the kind of individualism that cuts us off from life-giving relationships with others.

And when it comes to technology, Gen Z understands that the horse has left the barn and attempting to close the doors at this point won't do any good. Instead, we must work to make sure that our engagement with young people via social media and other technology is faithful, life-giving, and at the service of authentic relationships. Social media can be a powerful tool for pushing back against many of the messages with which Gen Z is nearly constantly bombarded. (Don't believe me? Just check out the cool things often going on with "Weird Catholic Twitter"[13] or the discussions that take place on numerous Catholic Discord servers.) Though physical and embodied relationships are absolutely essential, this generation is pushing the Church to up its game when it comes to how it projects the Gospel online.

Simply put, if we don't meet this generation in virtual spaces, we have little hope of meeting them in real spaces.

Finally, the focus Gen Z has on racial and other forms of justice can and should serve as a much-needed push for the Church to refocus itself on its own resources and teachings by reading the signs of the times. As Valdary's own vision of racial justice makes clear, we need not capitulate to ideologies that are hostile to a Catholic vision of the human person when doing this. But we need to zero in much more intently on the role that explicit and structural injustices have played in marginalizing those who most clearly bear the face of Christ as the least among us.

Indeed, given that Matthew 25 insists our very salvation depends on our giving special preference to these marginalized populations, the pushes Gen Z gives in this regard may save our souls.

Conclusion

"But wait," I can hear a skeptic saying, "Don't the woke Zoomers have views about race, gender, and sexual orientation that are at odds with the Church's teachings on the dignity of the human person? And don't they hold them so stridently that the difficult conversations this book is trying to facilitate are almost impossible to have?"

Maybe. But let's remind ourselves to distinguish between the performative virtual world of social media (from where much of the evidence for the above claim would come) and the real-life, embodied interactions among real people sharing the same real space. Recall, again, that Springtide found Gen Z is open to engaging with those who disagree with them.

The problem isn't that we cannot engage with younger people who disagree with the Church on these matters. The problem is that *we haven't demonstrated that we care about them*; that we are genuinely listening; that we want a relationship with them; that we welcome them—and that their Creator does the same but with a radical love and acceptance (along with forgiveness) that to the world seems like folly.

Before we dust off our trusty apologetic arguments about matters where we suspect there is disagreement, let us first convince Gen Z that we genuinely love them and want them to be part of a life-giving community. Once that trust and genuine connection are established, they will be able to see that the institutional Church is made up of people who see them as full persons, created "good" by God and bearing God's image and likeness in a unique way.

Yes, there is a time for engaging the justice-related issues that come so quickly to the lips (and fingertips) of Gen Z. (And there is good reason to be hopeful about such engagement—not least because, again, they largely don't know the rich tradition of the Church on these issues.) But there's another step, a foundational step, that comes first. They have to believe, *really believe*, that we see them as fellow bearers of the divine image.

Part III

CATHOLICS OF EVERY STRIPE

5

The Newbie Convert

I.e., "The Treasure Hunter"

1. The Thin Caricature

Can you believe there is even a thin caricature for new Catholic converts? It isn't openly discussed very often, but you've probably come across the caricature before. Indeed, maybe you've even been on the business end of it. These "newbie" or "know-it-all" Catholics seem to think they are "more Catholic than the pope"—which at the time I write this book includes being skeptical of (or even outright hostile to) the current Holy Father, Pope Francis.

Recent converts are enthusiastic about all things Catholic, but they haven't had the time to really grow and situate their perspectives with others in the Church who are more seasoned and more knowledgeable, that is, with those who have been around longer. Converts who come into the Church from evangelical backgrounds bring that fundamentalist style and approach into the Church. They go too much "by the book" and are too interested in simplistic, easy answers. Cradle Catholics, unburdened by this background, are often better able to embrace the complexity and ambiguity of the faith with more nuance. They know what it means to participate in the messiness of it all.

Many of these converts also bring their secular politics with them into the Church. The "Am I my brother's keeper?" libertarian mentality, for example, has no place in the Catholic Church. Of course, many converts don't understand, or may have never even been taught about, the Church's social teaching and the positive role the state can play in working toward the common good of all.

To the extent they are aware of it, they tend to dismiss its importance in comparison to the "pelvic issues" surrounding sexuality and reproduction that often have pride of place in motivating their conversion.

Overall, there is a sense in this caricature that newbie converts aren't really Catholic. Or they aren't really Catholic *yet*. They need to know their place, take some time to chill, listen, and learn from those of us who really know what's going on around here. There's a clear "us" and a clear "them."

2. What Is in Our Hearts?

This is the part of the chapter in which we get the chance to wonder if (or how) we are part of the problem. We attempt to humbly check our biases and see if we are seeking to limit or ignore God's working through—in this case—recent converts to the Catholic Church. We ask, again: "Are *we* the baddies?"

The main problem isn't that new converts struggle to understand what it means to be part of the Catholic Church. More often, it is that we prefer to ignore (or even dissent from) the very teachings and values that new converts find so attractive. Especially if we identify as more of a progressive Catholic, it can be really disconcerting when someone converts on the basis of ideas we wish were eradicated from the Church!

But this challenge doesn't come exclusively from progressive Catholics. A good number of converts over the last several years share Pope Francis's vision of Catholicism. They are focused on mercy, anti-clericalism, accompaniment, and an indefatigable emphasis on the poor and the stranger. They chose to become Catholic to be a part of a Church whose first reaction to "the world" is to become a field hospital—rather than one whose primary approach is one of intentional resistance, even antagonism.

And, let's be honest, there are likely some good old-fashioned group dynamics in play here as well. We've all been there when a new kid shows up (school, work, sports, etc.) and there's a clear expectation that they sit down, shut up, and do a lot of listening and dues-paying before they start yapping about whatever they happen to be thinking about. Also, the new kid should not be critiquing those who have been part of the group for much longer. They need to know their place.

The family dynamic, which is the way we should be thinking about the Church, often adds another layer to all of this. The "boss baby," newly arrived to the family, is well known for causing backlash and jealousy in older children. Dayton University theologian Kelly Johnson put it this way when speaking about Protestants joining the Catholic family: "Protestants were step-siblings who claimed they knew my father better than my mother did. Were they family or traitors? Could my father really love them, too? I was fascinated by them. I was jealous of them. I pitied them."[1] From the perspective of some of the "older kids," things in the family were just fine before our new sibling showed up, thank you. The Church was a comfortable and familiar place, and we wanted it to stay that way. The arrival of newbies upsets that comfort and familiarity.

But if one takes just a moment to flip through the Bible or the history of the Church, it isn't clear why anyone would expect that kind of stability. To name just the most prominent example, think about what happened when Saul of Tarsus became the Apostle Paul. He was certainly the new guy on the block and had some ideas that were quite different from what was going on in Jerusalem with Peter and the rest of those who had known Jesus in the flesh. But, with all respect to the Blues Brothers, he had quite literally been given a mission from God.

Predictably, a combination of Paul's being the new guy and his new and seemingly strange ideas ("What, you don't need to get circumcised anymore? And you can still eat shellfish? That's kooky talk!") rubbed many fellow Christians the wrong way.

Yet, even St. Peter himself, the very rock on which Christ built his Church, was forced to put aside his own biases and acknowledge that God was doing something new and essential through this newbie, Paul of Tarsus. (More on this in the conclusion to this chapter.) There's a dynamic in the Church that is different from, say, what we encounter at school or work. God can and does work through recent converts in a way that may surprise us. Indeed, this may even make us angry.

If we encounter these situations, it is our job to get ourselves out of the way and allow God to fully work through the newbies. In the story that follows, for example, it is very clear that God is able to work wonders through new converts.

3. A Story That Thickens

Sohrab Ahmari, living in the Islamic Iran of his childhood, came to know "god" in the form of "judicial amputations and floggings, scowling ayatollahs and secret police."[2] He grew up in a culture that lived one way of life in public, so as to avoid the attention of the theocratic authorities, and a different way in private. There was no place for love and mercy. If this was what "god" was like, a young and headstrong Ahmari "wanted nothing to do with him." He became an atheist at age thirteen.

Renouncing his faith, however, didn't stop his search for truth and meaning. Soon after immigrating to the United States with his parents and going to college, Ahmari began

going down a familiar path, uniting his atheism to Marxism—
an ideology that, when he looks back, was clearly unable to fill
his hunger for God. In his fantastic book *From Fire by Water*,
Ahmari explains how "a number of astonishing and quite
providential encounters with the Mass" were instrumental
in the initial stages of his conversion. He didn't know much
about the Church or about the supernatural graces associated
with Mass, but he notes that the "decisive" thing for his conversion was "our Lord's Eucharistic presence."

Ahmari is obviously not an ex-evangelical Christian, but
he still identifies as a traditional Catholic and a conservative. Indeed, he very often writes for a publication called *The
American Conservative*. On the basis of this, some have simply
assumed that he's not a fan of Pope Francis—but this is *absolutely* not the case. Time and time again, he makes his loyalty
known, especially on social media:

> All who follow me know how serious I am about
> loyalty to the Holy Father. Time and again, I've shot
> down the anti-Francis grifters.[3]

> A general reminder that if you call Pope Francis a
> "heretic," a "commie," etc., you will earn an auto-
> matic block from me—zero discussion.[4]

One of the major reasons Ahmari is so supportive of the
Holy Father, beyond the loyalty he owes him as the visible
head of the Church, is because he gets a central political issue
of our time correct, even as many who identify as conservative do not: freedom doesn't exist in a vacuum, but correctly understood, it directs us *toward* the good. Ahmari calls
out libertarians and other conservatives for whiffing on this
essential point. His story already blows up the caricature of
converts on multiple levels, but Ahmari's politics are especially
interesting in this regard. Instead of importing a foreign conservative vision into the Church, he's much more interested in

trying to persuade conservatives to see the truth and wisdom of Catholic social teaching. He's interested in pushing them to put the poor before the rich and labor before capital.

I think it is fair to say that the Marxist analysis of his college days still lingers within him, especially when he explains to fellow conservatives that "class analysis is your friend."[5] Even more dramatically, he explicitly states that he wants "the GOP remade as a workers' party."[6] In this regard, he couldn't be more thrilled that major corporations seem to be more interested in working with Democrats than with Republicans.[7] Though perhaps painful in the short run because of fundraising, Ahmari's view would support that weening ourselves from an addiction to corporate money is the only way to reflect Catholic political values. Indeed, it frees us up to talk about the need to do all sorts of things that are in competition with corporate interests, for example, supporting labor unions, regulating markets, increasing wages, and more.

4. What Are the Gifts and Truths Being Proclaimed?

If Ahmari is guilty of anything, it is that he has smuggled the Church's social teaching into the world of Catholic political conservatism that sometimes ignores it or even dissents from it. At the same time, he also energetically supports the Church's teaching on the so-called pelvic issues—and, indeed, sees no artificial right/left divide between the two.

And that's one of the great gifts many recent converts bring with them to the Church. They are often choosing to be a member of the Church *in its fullness*. Rather than ignoring essential aspects of a Catholic vision of the good, they offer Catholics a chance to take a second look at matters they either have rejected or thought they had perfectly figured out.

Speaking personally now, I used to be the kind of cradle Catholic who—while I never wavered on my pro-life views— basically jettisoned most of what the Church had to say about something like contraception. Most of the folks in my cradle Catholic circles did the same, and we talked to each other often about how the Church's teaching on contraception was obviously outdated and false. It was only after several encounters with faithful, educated, and holy converts to the faith that I slowly began to rethink these positions. Without their commitment to the fullness of the faith, I certainly wouldn't be writing a book like this. Heck, I'm not sure I'd even be a Catholic theologian at all.

What a gift to the Church these converts are! They remind cradle Catholics—who can all too easily identify with one faction or another—that the Gospel of Jesus Christ proclaimed by his Church cannot be made to fit into human-created categories.

Many of us think of the Catholic Church as still being dogged by the scandal of the sex abuse crisis. And there is obviously a good reason for this. While major progress has been made as the Church continues to reckon with its past and do a better job to protect children and other vulnerable people going into the future, the dramatic and indefensible failures—including a failure of restorative justice that goes beyond mere financial payouts—still loom large in the broader culture.

The *New York Times* thought it was so remarkable when, in 2019, "thousands of people converted to Catholicism" in an "age of scandal" that they decided to do a feature article on this topic.[8] In the process of researching the article, they discovered more gifts that converts offer the Church. One woman attended Mass with her Catholic daughters and gradually, over years, was drawn into the faith. Another man went on a spiritual quest—speaking with imams, rabbis, and priests, and eventually chose the Church, despite the friction it was likely going to cause with his broader family. And one woman, when asked by the reporter whether her decision to convert would be "linked to the sex abuse scandal," had this very informed and mature response: "The Church has been here two thousand years. It has withstood scandal upon scandal, crusades, political upheaval, and yet it still exists. There's a greater presence at work."

For many cradle Catholics, the sex abuse crisis plays into their particular and long-standing frustrations with the Church: celibate clergy, a gay subculture among certain priests and seminarians, and a hierarchy that is obsessed with keeping power from the laity, among others. But for this convert mentioned in the *New York Times* article and many others like her, they can see an admittedly horrific scandal within the broader historical context of many other horrific scandals. And perhaps they can see this more clearly because they are not tempted to use the sex abuse scandal as a means of advancing a particular agenda. Free of this baggage and inclination, they are perhaps also free to see God's presence guiding his Church throughout it all.

Because these newbies are convinced of God's working within the Church at a foundational level, the Holy Spirit leads them to convert even when it puts their close familial relationships at risk. Such witness can be essential for lukewarm, autopilot, "meh" Catholics who are happy to live a culturally accommodating life in which something other than the Gospel proclaimed by the Church is their source of ultimate concern.

Converts can help shake cradle Catholics out of this kind of slumber and awaken them to the truth, beauty, and love that Christ and his Church have to offer when we make a commitment to put them first in our lives.

5. What Are the Challenges?

Like all the groups we are engaging, there are often profound challenges faced by new converts. Sometimes, with a bit of time to marinate in the family of the Church, the converts themselves can identify these challenges quite clearly. One of those converts is Sohrab Ahmari, as evidenced by his answer to the following question I asked him in the pages of *Crux* magazine:

> Me: As you no doubt know, some cradle Catholics criticize Catholic converts for thinking of membership in the Church as an (often uncritical) assent to a set of propositions—rather than, say, being welcomed as a new member of a family with lots of diversity and often hard differences. How do you react to such criticism?
>
> Ahmari: You know, I think there is something to these criticisms. And it's an especially dangerous temptation among writers and intellectuals who convert. I'm ashamed when I think back to my period of instruction and first few months as a baptized and confirmed Catholic, when I thought that, having read some important books and memorized a few of the necessary prayers in Latin, I could pronounce with authority on ecclesial debates. What vanity! It's only now, more than two years since I was received, that I'm beginning to understand what being part of that great family—reaching across heaven, earth, and purgatory, with Christ as our head—is all about.[9]

What an honest, thoughtful, and truthful reflection from Ahmari—one that I hope other new converts can hear!

Newbies have many gifts to offer the Church, and the Church needs those gifts desperately. But some new converts need to "slow their roll" and understand that, though they are truly a full member of the Catholic family, there is still more to understand about how the Church works. The process they are going through is difficult to explain, but maybe it is kind of like being an adopted child or a stepchild in a family. They are not only legally and intentionally a full part of a new family but also adapting to a situation they do not yet completely grasp. Again, the new arrivals have their own gifts to offer this family, and those will fully shine through with time, but the prudent thing to do at first is to listen and learn.

Part of the caricature that rings true is that new converts sometimes do have a simplistic view of what it means to be a part of their new family. It is possible for any Catholic—new or longtime—to hold views that put one outside the family of the Church. But what that means in any given case is often extremely complex. This is especially true, as we have already seen, when we honor the healthy tension in the Church between following our personal conscience and assenting to the current teaching of the Church. This gets even more complex when we think about various prudential judgments and how they are applied to numerous important public issues.

I can illustrate with the recent example of the intra-Catholic debate in some quarters about the COVID-19 vaccines and their relationship to elective abortion. If one comes into the faith without having fully absorbed (or, in some cases, without even hearing about) the Church's nuanced understanding of cooperation with evil, then it can be extremely puzzling to understand why the pope, the Congregation of the Doctrine of the Faith, the US Conference of Catholic Bishops, and the National Catholic Bioethics Center would all clearly state that use of COVID-19 vaccines were morally licit for Catholics, even though they had been tested on cloned cell lines that could be traced back to an abortion in the Netherlands in the 1970s.

In such contexts, it can be tempting for converts to barge into the debate, full of understandable and (frankly) awesome pro-life energy and insist that Catholics ought not to take the vaccine. But this was one of those situations in which it would have been prudent for new converts with this view to pause, take a look around, listen to those who have already been marinated in a Catholic vision, think hard and prayerfully about what they have to say, and only then enter the fray.

6. Opportunities for Unity-in-Diversity

The teaching of the Church, as always, provided unity when it came to the response to the vaccines. But the diversity pushed by several converts on the very same issue was also profound. Many of them witnessed to the fact that the only vaccines available were morally compromised and that this was a profound tragedy. They reminded us that we should take them, not with a feeling of pure relief and celebration but with a somber acknowledgment that the drug we are putting in our bodies was tested on the cloned cells of a baby tragically and horrifically killed in abortion—and that we should be pushing for better alternatives in the production of future drugs.

This reminds us of one of the great general gifts of diversity that new Catholic converts often bring to the Church. While at times it is very important to listen to the wisdom that the world has to offer, cradle Catholics should admit that we can often be more interested in social acceptance than putting the teaching of Christ and his Church at the center of our lives. Catholic conformists who uncritically follow the "spirit of the age" often need the very kick in the pants that a new convert, on fire for the faith, can helpfully give them.

Indeed, the Great Commission that Christ gives us all—to make disciples of all nations—is often lost on self-satisfied Catholics who can't be bothered to share the truth they have been given with anyone else. New converts, by contrast, are often so grateful for the treasure they find in the Catholic Church that they are more likely to push the broader Church to share God's gifts with others.

Kelly Johnson puts the unity-in-diversity relationship beautifully: "We may find that new Catholics, free of memory and all the baggage of anger and grief that builds up among those who are Catholics since childhood, simply do not see the Church as we do. It may be that they are still in the honeymoon period and can learn from those of us who are more seasoned; it may also be that they can appreciate our mother as we, who have taken her for granted all our lives, do not."[10]

Conclusion

The tension between the old guard who have "been around" and get the complexities and nuances of the Church and newbie converts has been present since the first decades of the Church's existence. As we recalled earlier, differences arose between the original apostles and new Christian converts, especially between James, head of the so-called Judaizing Christians in Jerusalem, and Paul, leader of the movement bringing Gentiles into the Christian fold.

It is a bit more complex than this, but folks on James's side were certainly annoyed by these new disciples who didn't seem to get that fidelity to the Jewish law was an inherent part of what it meant to be a follower of Christ. Meanwhile, those on Paul's side, very new to the community and full of energy, couldn't understand why the old guard wouldn't make space for all the new converts who were not raised Jewish and who had little understanding of Jewish law.

One can imagine what a hard sell it must have been to ancient Greek and Roman Gentiles that in order to follow Christ one had to get circumcised and give up shellfish and pork. From the perspective of Paul and company, folks like James needed to be shaken from their dogmatic slumber so that they could see more clearly what God was doing with this new Jesus movement.

Both the old guard and the newbies had important points to make in the first-century Church. As with today, the tension was real and the disagreement was sharp, but it was also healthy. It is essential that the Church resist being corrupted by the spirit of the age, but it is equally important that the Church be open to understanding when God is doing something new. Living in that place of tension honors God's voice spoken in ages past while at the same time honoring God's voice speaking to us today.

What about when there is not just tension but also contradiction? The early church called a meeting of their leadership, the so-called Council of Jerusalem (Acts 15), and listened to all those who had differences. The result was making space for different ways while heeding the essentials of the faith that united them. To be Christian in Jerusalem could be quite different in many ways from being Christian in Corinth.

And how do we know what those unifying essentials were? The teaching of the Church as inspired by the Holy Spirit is the unity that makes the diversity possible.

6

The Single-Issue Pro-Life Activist

I.e., "The Human Rights Warrior"

1. The Thin Caricature

What image comes to your mind when someone says, "single-issue pro-life activist"?

Perhaps you think of—stop me if you're heard this reference before—an older white male, someone "obsessed with controlling women's bodies." Maybe you think of a Republican "who only cares about babies before they are born."

You might also think of this person as hopelessly incoherent in their views. They are skeptical of government intervention in every other area except, of course, when it comes to controlling women's bodies. If Catholic, they are interested in imposing the Church's teaching prohibiting abortion onto others who disagree. But if pressed on addressing the social teaching of the Church on other matters, what do we get from them? Crickets. Their political commitments oppose the pro-life goals of everything from paying workers a living wage to providing universal health care for the very women they want to control—even when doing so might save the lives of the babies they claim to value and would certainly help the children single mothers already have.

Their real goals have nothing to do with abortion. But they are happy to use babies as human shields—essentially as cover for advancing conservative/libertarian political agendas. Theirs is a classic but particularly disgusting example of idolatry.

Maybe the best examples of this, so the caricature goes, are Republican pro-life legislators. Pennsylvania representative Timothy Murphy, for instance, was a charter member of the Republican pro-life caucus in Washington, DC—that is, until his own infidelity meant that he'd need abortion to cover his tracks. Then he was all about pressuring the woman with whom he had an affair to have an abortion she didn't want to have. And when she pressed him on how he could do such a thing when he would publicly tout very pro-life messages, he responded by saying, "I've never written them. Staff does them. I read them and winced."[1]

"But what about the *true* believers?" you ask. Well, in this caricature, they are almost all radicals, even violent radicals. Rather than trust women and respect their bodily autonomy, they are the kinds of people who would get in their faces and yell at them to "keep their legs closed" (or some such dismissive phrase) and try to convert them to a narrow-minded, pelvic-issue-obsessed version of Catholicism. A good percentage are explicitly OK with doing violence to abortion clinics—and even killing doctors in the name of their extremist ideology.

No one should call these people "pro-lifers." A much better phrase is "anti-choicers." Or maybe "forced-birthers." At best—at our most generous—we can call them "abortion foes." They are certainly not pro-life, far, far from it.

2. What Is in Our Hearts?

More often than we like to admit (and perhaps, if we are being honest, most of the time?), the things that bother us in other people are the things we don't like in ourselves.

There is something true to be found in the caricature. But in this case, the problem of political idolatry in our abortion discourse is with both those who identify with the Catholic right and those who identify with the Catholic left.

We will discuss this more below, but let's admit up front that political idolatry abounds among pro-life Catholic conservatives. But for those of us who are making the caricature, what about our own political idolatry? What would have to change about our political affiliations if we took the views of the single-issue pro-life activist seriously? In addition:

- What if we acknowledged the horrific truth that hundreds of thousands of the most vulnerable children imaginable are killed each year in the United States?

- What if we absorbed the fact that unborn children are killed not only because a desperate mother was facing poverty but also because her boyfriend threatened to beat her up or kill her if she didn't have an abortion?

- What if we realized that parents, teachers, and other mentors fill students' heads with the message that they can never have a happy or successful life if they have a child while single?

- What if we remember that there are human traffickers and pimps who force women to have abortions?

- What if we consider that doctors often make dire predictions of hardships to expectant parents who find out they will have a child with Down syndrome?

- And what if you absorbed the fact that the Democratic Party, and the political left in the United States more broadly, now push abortion not as a necessary evil to be limited but as a fundamental, unlimited right and even a social good?[2]

If we really absorbed all these things, some of us would have to fundamentally rethink our politics. It would seem obvious that no party that directly advocates for such evil could have our support. Substitute "toddlers" or "Black people" in the placeholder for prenatal children, and the kind of violence we're talking about here would make any party that defended and supported it instantly unsupportable.

But for those of us who have made an idol out of left-wing politics (and right-wing politics are no better!), the views of the single-issue pro-life activist simply have to be wrong. Otherwise, their entire political universe falls apart. Rather than having their actual arguments engaged, such pro-life activists must be dismissed as extremists, fanatics, and basically anything that makes them "the other." This is certainly not treating them as fellow Christians who, because of their Baptism, should be thought of first as part of our family.

3. A Story That Thickens

What you just read wasn't very hopeful. The story of Obianuju Ekeocha is just the opposite. Ekeocha, for reasons mentioned above, is often dismissed as a single-issue pro-life activist. An international figure, she's been invited to speak at the White House, the State Department, and several colleges and universities. In a recent talk at Notre Dame, for instance, she gave a groundbreaking lecture on reproductive health and the rise of ideological neocolonialism—arguing that the Western world (led by the United States) is intentionally destroying the reproductive cultures and values of developing countries.

Obianuju Ekeocha grew up in Nigeria and experienced this firsthand. Though she is best known for her founding and advocacy of an authentically African pro-life organization, Culture of Life Africa,[3] her day job is working as a biomedical scientist in hematology. Indeed, she says it was an experience she had working in a Western hospital that shocked her conscience into realizing what was going on.[4] She was raised, she says, in a pro-life society that did not have legal abortion. Her native language doesn't even have a word for *abortion* that doesn't have a negative connotation associated with it. Abortion is a taboo concept in her culture. But when working in a London hospital, she was forced to confront the fact that "wanted babies" were being born in one room while "in the next room, a baby was being killed."

As a result of this experience, she began her journey as a human rights warrior. Ekeocha didn't burst onto the public scene until she saw Melinda Gates launching what she now recognizes as a Western neocolonial reproductive project designed to limit the population of Africa. In response to Gates, she wrote an open letter calling this out.[5] Africans needed not Western-style views of population control but rather support for their cultural value of loving and welcoming babies.

Ekeocha boldly told Gates that if she genuinely wished to "listen to the heart-felt cry of an African woman," then she should "mercifully channel her funds to pay for what we *really* need." And then she provided a list of needs:

- Improved health-care systems (especially prenatal, neo-natal, and pediatric care);
- food programs for young children;
- higher education opportunities;
- chastity programs;
- support for micro-business opportunities for women; and
- fortification of already established nongovernmental organizations that are aimed at protecting women from sex trafficking, prostitution, forced marriage, child labor, domestic violence, sex crimes, and more.

A lifelong Catholic, Ekeocha grounds her beliefs in Church teaching, especially from encyclicals like *Humanae Vitae* and *Evangelium Vitae*. But that doesn't cut her off at all from the teachings of the Church that, at least in an American context, are considered "leftist" or "progressive." Indeed, the term *neocolonialism* itself is mostly invoked in academic and activist circles on the left—but she uses it (correctly) to undermine the basic assumptions of these same folks, turning their own critique against them.[6]

Though she has views that could lead her to be dismissed as a "single-issue pro-life activist and certainly doesn't speak for all Black American Catholics," Ekeocha herself blows up the caricature. As you've no doubt figured out by this point, she isn't an "old white male." She obviously isn't some kind of libertarian who doesn't think the government has a role to play in supporting women and those who are economically vulnerable. Though she gives preeminent priority to abortion, she is pro-life in a much broader sense as well. She is a human rights warrior.

4. What Are the Gifts and Truths Being Proclaimed?

Obianuju Ekeocha gives the Church an incredible gift. She and others like her focus our attention specifically on the most vulnerable human beings of all, prenatal children.

And you know who agrees with Ekeocha and other pro-lifers? Pope Francis.

Yes, the Holy Father strongly insists that abortion is a fundamental violation of human rights.[7] Some mistakenly believe that in one of the first interviews of his pontificate Francis actually asked Catholics to downplay abortion. But if we read his words in context it is clear that he, like Ekeocha, wants to put abortion first in the context of other human rights.[8] Indeed, in a profoundly inconvenient move for those who wish to use that interview to give less weight to abortion, the very next day Pope Francis insisted in a speech to OB-GYNs in Rome that "every unborn child, though unjustly condemned to be aborted, has the face of the Lord."[9]

And this is not the only time Pope Francis has spoken up so clearly on behalf of prenatal children. Using language that is more hardcore than any of his predecessors, Francis has called abortion a "white gloved Nazi crime" and even compared abortion to the hiring of a hitman. He has advocated, especially in his home country of Argentina, to defend the human rights of this most vulnerable population with the force of law, something that prenatal justice requires.[10]

The reaction of the pro-choice Argentinian health minister Ginés González García to the views of Pope Francis and other pro-lifers unintentionally and interestingly reveals what is at stake when it comes to prenatal justice. She said:

> Here there are not two lives as some say. There's clearly a single person and the other is a phenomenon. If it were not like that, we would be facing the greatest universal genocide, [because] more than half the civilized world allows it.[11]

What a remarkable self-own by the health minister! If we take Obianuju Ekeocha, Pope Francis, and other Catholic human rights warriors seriously, then we must admit that the violence that threatens these children (who, again, bear the face of Christ in a special way) is a kind of genocide. Considering this type of horrific mass violence, it is not only understandable but also absolutely required that the US bishops make abortion a preeminent focus of their justice-centered interventions.

Still skeptical? Let's put the death abortion causes into perspective. In 2020 and 2021, abortion killed hundreds of thousands more people than did the COVID-19 pandemic. And that is not at all to minimize the pandemic! The dramatic things we did as a culture to lower the COVID-19 death toll challenges us to take a similarly dramatic approach to lowering the horrific mass death that abortion brings to our culture, year in and year out. Recent legal cases, including *Dobbs v. Jackson,* which returned the decision of abortion to the states, provide some hope of moving the culture more firmly in the direction of prenatal justice.

The normalization of abortion has made many of us numb and complacent. That is why the gifts of human rights warriors are so important. They are willing to take the stinging criticism and the marginalization of themselves from the halls of respectability in order to remind us of the central focus Catholics must have on prenatal justice. They are the voice of God begging us to join them in becoming a voice for the (literally) voiceless.

5. What Are the Challenges?

Hear me out: the best approaches to saving lives during the pandemic attacked the problem and used multiple effective strategies without letting politics get in the way. Yes, masks and physical distancing were important, but so was getting outside and getting enough vitamin D. Yes, it was important (for the vulnerable especially) to get vaccinated, but it was also important to have access to antiviral therapies for those who did get infected, and so on.

But just as our horrifically polarized politics kept good people from taking an "all of the above" approach during the pandemic, similar political forces keep good people from taking an "all of the above" approach to abortion.

If we are going to resist a throwaway culture that considers prenatal children expendable, then yes, working for their equal protection under the law is an essential part of what we must be about. This is simply what justice requires. And it must be said that one of our two major political parties is friendly to this position, while the other major party is actively hostile to it.

It also must be said that pro-life Catholics are in the business of defending human dignity—advocating on behalf of the most vulnerable—in ways that go beyond legal protection to active support. This is why so many pro-lifers contribute to (and even run) pregnancy help centers for vulnerable women. They aren't just interested in reducing the "supply" of abortion by making it less available; they are interested in *reducing the demand* for abortion—something that they know will still exist even if abortion is made broadly illegal.

A challenge comes into play here. While many so-called single-issue pro-lifers understandably feel more comfortable working with Republicans, there is a risk that support could turn into an idol. And that idolatry has the potential to distort their perspective not only on the many other pro-life issues on which the Church speaks (for example, things like ecological concern and welcoming refugees). It could even distort their perspective on prenatal justice itself.

Virtually no one likes abortion. That's what makes the current Democratic Party's position so utterly heinous. Most women end up having abortions that they really don't want to have. Indeed, studies have found a strong correlation between abortion and "intimate partner violence," especially when a woman has had multiple abortions.[12] But even more often, abortion coercion is less explicit and based on the social pressures a woman is facing.

Consider this evidence from the *New York Times*: "The gap between the number of children that women say they want to have (2.7) and the number of children they will probably actually have (1.8) has risen to the highest level in 40 years."[13] And here are some of the most important reasons listed in the article women gave for this gap:

- "Childcare is too expensive" (64 percent)
- "Worried about the economy" (49 percent)
- "Can't afford more children" (44 percent)
- "Not enough paid family leave" (39 percent)
- "No paid family leave" (38 percent)

Human rights warriors should focus on lowering the things that increase demand for abortion by supporting social programs that, though very consistent with Catholic social teaching, are not consistent with the current ethos of the Republican Party. Paid family leave, help with childcare, and housing policies that avoid the two-income trap should be fully considered because they can all be used to save the lives of babies and support women. Anything less than an "all of the above strategy" in moving toward this goal is unacceptable. It is *egregiously unacceptable* if we are not doing it because we are more loyal to the approach of a particular secular political party than we are to what should be a much more foundational goal.

6. Opportunities for Unity-in-Diversity

Our primary concern should be to live out the fullness of our Catholic faith without this kind of political idolatry. Yet even with this difficult issue, we must still be consistent with the "different strokes for different folks" way of being a family. We are one body but many parts. An arm has a particular role to play, as do the lungs, as do the feet, and so on.

Human rights warriors who are locked on prenatal justice as their issue are performing an essential function within the Body of Christ. Others may be more focused on racism, euthanasia, homelessness, education, capital punishment, or any number of issues. The key is that this diversity of focus is united in the communal, unifying vision of the good proclaimed by Christ and his Church.

To be one with the Church, the Body of Christ, means that we must be doing everything we can to avoid making an idol out of a particular secular political program. On one hand, we must welcome those who are often dismissed as single-issue pro-lifers as essential members of the Catholic family. On the other hand, this means human rights warriors locked on abortion must use all the tools at their disposal for protecting and supporting the lives of prenatal children and their mothers. That is, they must not become comfortable sticking with any one secular party's political program for pursuing prenatal justice. This will require these human rights warriors to be more agile in their politics. In one moment, they may be called to work with Republicans to pass laws that protect prenatal children. But in another moment, they may be called to work with Democrats to pass laws that offer social support to women and children.

Happily, we are currently in a time of ferment and creativity within American politics. I know we're never supposed to mention Donald Trump in a positive context—and I could never vote for him—but let's admit that US political categories have been scrambled since his election. And they have been scrambled in ways that create openings for Catholics to be more nimble in their political approaches.

We might emulate the Democratic governor of Louisiana, John Bel Edwards, who has both signed a bill banning abortion after a prenatal baby's heartbeat can be detected *and* bucked the trend of red southern states by expanding his state's Medicaid program under the Affordable Care Act. We could also look to Senator Marco Rubio and his "common good conservativism," which is all about prenatal justice but not afraid to use government programs (such as paid family leave[14]) as social support for women.

Significantly, a whopping 44 percent of Americans refuse to identify with either major party and instead describe themselves as "independents."[15] This number dwarfs those who identify as Democrats or Republicans—which means Catholics who refuse to identify with either party are in good company!

Conclusion

Does some of what I'm proposing here seem too pie-in-the-sky? Too disconnected from a political reality so infected with idolatry?

I can understand this reaction. No one should be unclear about the kind of work it will take to undo the ideological damage this chapter has addressed. But here's some good news: examples of what I'm calling for here have already occurred.

Remember how the Republicans, just after Trump's election, decided to amend the tax code to make sure that the government wasn't "picking winners and losers"? What that meant in practice was that tax incentives would disappear for many good things that Catholics are bound to support including, unbelievably, the tax credit that was going to adoptive parents.

Personally, I'm quite biased here as my wife and I could have only afforded to adopt our three oldest children with the help of this tax credit. I, therefore, joined many other pro-lifers in firmly criticizing the libertarian-minded Republicans who wanted to do this.[16] And you know what? We won! The pressure we put on got the tax credit back into the bill.[17]

Thank God we did. Providing the genuine option to choose adoption is one of the most important anti-abortion, pro-life, human rights–centered things we can do. And truth be told, we need more work to make adoption more available as an option—including by reducing adoption stigma and offering support to families who struggle to meet the special challenges that adoption involves.

That's only one example, obviously. But it is an important one—not only because of the priority of the issue itself but also because it shows what we can do if we buck political idolatry and fight for the fullness of our vision of the good.

7

The Progressive Professor

I.e., "The Challenging Mentor"

1. The Thin Caricature

Progressive Catholic professors. Do you know the type?

Imagine someone who tells you with a straight face that they are working on behalf of the marginalized and who wholeheartedly insists on a preferential option for the poor as they speak to their privileged colleagues in a fancy, chandelier-bedecked hotel ballroom in downtown Chicago.

Oh, and imagine someone who claims to be working on behalf of the Church while actually undermining Roman Catholicism by putting obstacle after obstacle in front of their faithful students. Upperclassmen at Notre Dame when I went there (which was way back in the mid-'90s!) would say "come to Notre Dame and lose your faith" for a reason. And it is even worse in Catholic higher education today.

As ostensibly Catholic theology departments slide into courses of study that are more history, psychology, or sociology than theology, and as Catholic colleges and universities hire professors with vague and free-floating appeals to "social justice" or "equity," the idea that there is any relationship to the Church at all becomes suspect. We may have a host of reasons to wonder whether our Catholic institutions of higher learning are Catholic at all.

Instead, the dominant ideology of the theology department and the university is the real source of authority, especially when it comes to (you guessed it!) gender identity and sexual orientation. What the Catholic Church teaches on these matters is not only not given a fair hearing; it is dismissed as outdated, obviously false, and evil. Presenting the Catholic position on these issues is treated as if it is giving a platform to a view that "erases the humanity" of self-identifying gay, lesbian, bisexual, and transgender persons. How can we expect them to engage points that are utterly hostile to their very existence?

"We don't give platforms to white supremacists," the progressive professor reminds us. "So why should we give them to transphobic and homophobic thinkers?"

It would be bad enough if there was nothing authentically Catholic about institutions dominated by today's progressive professors. But it is worse than this: authentic Catholicism is often explicitly and harshly opposed.

The net effect of this is that Catholic progressive academia can serve as a cover or front for Catholic institutions of higher learning that actually worship at the altar of different and false ideologies. Catholic social teachings (or Pope Francis's words from plane press conferences!) that appear to support these ideologies may sometimes be invoked to keep up appearances, but most other teachings of the Church are attacked as unjust and harmful.

Anyone who wants their kids educated in the faith should obviously keep them far, far away from institutions dominated by progressive Catholic professors.

2. What Is in Our Hearts?

As someone who has spent many years in the theology departments of Catholic universities, I know the caricature is pretty harsh. What's in the hearts of those who make it?

Let's begin by reminding ourselves about our current political moment: the cable news you watch and/or the folks you follow on social media almost certainly give you a profoundly biased understanding of, well, just about everything that is important, including what's happening in Catholic (and other) universities.

Happily, at least in my circles, more and more is being said about the "nut-picking" fallacy. What this refers to is that often those in various biased media focus on "nutty" or extreme figures in order to paint a false picture of an entire group. If you think all Catholic progressive professors are like the caricature above, you may be a victim of nut-picking. Sorry about that. You certainly aren't alone.

And here's another part of the picture to consider: progressive professors know more about theology than the average Catholic. That imbalance of knowledge can put one on the defensive, especially if the professor is challenging something that one holds dear. It can be difficult to listen to "hard truths"—on everything from the history of the Church to the sex abuse crisis—if they challenge us at the heart of our faith.

For those who want clear, easy, tight, formulaic answers to all their most important questions and who want their relationship with the Church to give them utter certainty in an uncertain world, progressive professors remind them that they can't have it. And this is deeply uncomfortable.

Did I mention discomfort? Progressive professors can make many different kinds of Catholics uncomfortable. Many make a career of it.

3. A Story That Thickens

At first glance, one might be tempted to dismissively put Julie Hanlon Rubio in a progressive Catholic professor box. She teaches on the Berkeley, California, campus of Santa Clara University's Jesuit School of Theology. (*Berkeley, California,* and *Jesuit* in one sentence is certain to raise some alarms!) Before that, she taught theology for nineteen years at the Jesuit Saint Louis University with a secondary appointment in Women's and Gender Studies. Yes, I said *Women's and Gender Studies.*

A self-described "child of Vatican II" who likes a good guitar Mass, her two major early-career influences were Elisabeth Schüssler Fiorenza and David Hollenbach, two figures cut right out of the progressive professor cloth.[1]

Her current book project with Oxford University Press is titled *Catholic and Feminist: Is It Still Possible?* and past projects include a volume coedited with Charles Curran, one of the most important figures in the world of progressive Catholic theology. Given her relationship with Curran, who famously dissented from the Church's teaching on artificial contraception, one might not be surprised to find Rubio questioning the Church about its position on this issue.[2]

A final piece of evidence for putting Rubio into the progressive Catholic professor box might be her views on same-sex marriage. She foregrounds the views of Catholic progressive theologians such as Margaret Farley who argue that same-sex couples have the same moral obligations to each other and to the common good.[3] Plus, Rubio argues that "experience" reveals that the Church's teaching on the irreducibility of the male/female distinction makes this issue "more complicated than you think."[4] Indeed, the way things "strike" her when she encounters same-sex couples leads her to question "the import of the male/female distinction."

But even here, on this set of issues, we can thicken out Professor Rubio's story in ways that push back against the lazy caricature. Though I strongly suspect she doesn't agree with the Church's teaching on same-sex marriage, she doesn't publicly and aggressively contradict the teaching either. Instead, she focuses on asking questions and engaging complexities.

Indeed, she is careful to note that "experience alone never solves a problem in Catholic moral theology" and that the issue has to be considered against the weight of "scripture, tradition, and the natural order." Indeed, much to her credit, she writes:

> The centrality of male-female partnership from Genesis forward cannot be denied. Essentially, the biblical argument is the natural law argument; what God wants for us is inscribed in our bodies and our natures. This is what Catholics whose experience suggests the validity of same sex marriage must confront.[5]

Far from censorious or hostile, Rubio has written an entire book on finding common ground across ideological differences.[6] And she has put her money where her mouth is on this issue on multiple occasions—even arguing that former Republican congressman Paul Ryan deserved a fair hearing in his confirmation as Speaker of the House and wide latitude when using his prudential judgment to come up with economic policies in light of Catholic social teaching.[7] These were Ryan-supported policies, to be clear, with which Rubio herself disagreed. Yet she took the time to engage in dialogues that involved "learning things" from libertarian economists that "I don't learn in my usual circles."[8]

Further, in a move that demonstrates her true colors, Rubio publicly argued that progressive theologians at the Catholic Theological Society of America should "embrace your conservative colleagues" with the goal of welcoming more ideological diversity into a community of scholars that very much lacks it.[9] Maybe more important, Rubio has publicly called out the Catholic Theological Society of America for very often discussing a preferential option for the poor amid the chandeliers. For much of her career she's used her

limited time to attend the annual meeting of the College Theology Society, a group that meets on college campuses, stays
in dorms, and eats cafeteria food. The *horror*.

4. What Are the Gifts and Truths Being Proclaimed?

Even if we are predisposed to be skeptical of and uncomfortable with progressive Catholic professors because we hold
strong views many of them tend to attack, what might happen if we made the effort to see the image of God in them?
What if we listened with humility and committed ourselves
to be the first to love? What if we paid attention to power and
how it functions within theology departments at Catholic
universities?

With regard to the second consideration, it is worth
mentioning that Professor Rubio has taken her path at great
personal risk to her career—and, indeed, may have put
herself out of the running for the kinds of prestigious jobs
that are consistent with her amazing publishing record. So,
here's the first thing to keep in mind: there is *tremendous*
pressure on many Catholic professors today to conform to
secular ideological orthodoxies of the academy—at least
if they want to become or remain respected within their
fields. For professors who are more traditional in their
views (or who even take seriously those who hold more
traditional views), showing up at most academic conferences is, well, becoming more and more awkward. You
might think of it like showing up to a Star Wars convention
dressed as Mr. Spock awkward.

With this background in place, might there be any space
to turn from dismissing a progressive Catholic professor as
merely ideological to thinking and maybe accepting him
or her as a "challenging mentor"? Those of us who believe
we worship a God who is the source of—oh, I don't know,
truth?—should not shrink from higher-level discussions in

pursuit of that truth. Becoming more aware of the truth can only draw us closer to our Father and Creator. Again, even if it makes us uncomfortable.

A classic example of this kind of commitment is one that St. Robert Bellarmine, a cardinal of the Church, exhibited in response to the challenge he faced from Galileo. Despite the fact that the upstart astronomer had not proven his case and was asking the Church to change its centuries-long position in favor of a heliocentric universe, Bellarmine responded to Galileo with a willingness to change his mind in light of new evidence:

> If there were a true demonstration that the sun is at the center of the world and the earth in the third heaven, and that the sun does not circle the earth but the earth circles the sun, then one would have to proceed with great care in explaining the Scriptures that appear contrary; and say rather that we do not understand them than that what is demonstrated is false. But I will not believe that there is such a demonstration, until it is shown me.[10]

Do we encounter Galileos in life? Yes, they might be arrogant, dismissive, and not (yet) have proven their case. But can we learn to be as generous as St. Robert Bellarmine, offer a fair hearing, and be prepared to enter into a more complex reality of our faith?

I'm just one person, of course, but this was very much my own experience. Before I got into higher education and studied Catholic theology in earnest, I had a very simplistic faith in the Church. I was lucky to have challenging mentors who took the time to disabuse me of my false beliefs, including and especially about what the Church historically thought about, among other things, the following:

- the moral status of the prenatal human being from conception;
- how Christ is present in the Eucharist;
- the development of the concept of marriage;
- Christian participation in the military;
- administration of the death penalty; and
- religious freedom and freedom of conscience more generally.

Many issues that are absolutely central for the Church today—as well as for my own Catholic faith—have had an interesting and complex story in getting to that central place. It will do us no good to have a naïve view of how the teachings of the Church developed over time. Indeed, if our faith is based on a historically false vision of the Church, then it is like a house built on sand. When the rain, winds, and floods come (and they will!), our personal faith will not stand.

We, therefore, shouldn't be afraid to have challenging mentors keeping us informed and honest about these matters. Even if we don't fully agree with everything they stand for, we should consider ourselves lucky to have people who force us to up our intellectual game and articulate better, more informed reasons for why we hold the views we do.

There is really a different perspective to the "come to Notre Dame and lose your faith" comment. I did basically lose my faith after having it challenged. But, frankly, it wasn't a faith worth keeping. It was a faith that wasn't dealing honestly with the truth. But once I rediscovered my faith, once I worked through those problems and found a community that helped me rebuild on solid ground, my faith was much, much stronger than it was before.

And I have challenging mentors to thank for it.

5. What Are the Challenges?

All that said, there are some real and profound challenges from and for progressive Catholic professors in our current moment. They not only wield the power to cancel those who think differently but also are starting to feel the same effects of cancel culture themselves.

Students remain on shakier ground. It is students who are putting grades and letters of recommendation (that is, their futures!) at risk if they speak up. But it is also true for faculty members who have differing points of view than their progressive colleagues. The publicly shared sense that one must conform to the new ideology or face serious consequences means many students and professors simply keep their heads down and hope the inquisitors (who, to push the analogy made above even further, are now properly part of the Star Wars canon) do not come for them.

The result is, to date, that authentic academic engagement across differences is attempted almost as frequently as the Chicago Bears win Super Bowls. Those are the kinds of things that used to be plausible back in the '80s. When so many Catholic professors focus only on wielding power in pursuit of an ideology, they undermine the very nature of the free and open inquiry in pursuit of truth that is at the heart of the academic project itself. Even worse, if the dominant ideology is hostile to the Church, Catholic academics are pushed more and more to use standards for their discipline that are also hostile.

Increasingly, higher education that brands itself as Catholic is nothing of the kind. Again, Church teaching on certain issues may be invoked when they are consistent with the secular spirit of the age, but very central ideas about justice are ignored altogether or even strongly opposed. The near complete whiff from progressive Catholic professors on a preeminent issue of our time—prenatal justice—has been an absolute disgrace. And I don't think we can be honest here if we didn't name "sex, gender, and reproduction" as particular sources of neuralgia.

Actually, that's not quite right. For those students and professors who have the "wrong" views on such topics, it is understood that they will keep silent and not rock the boat. So there actually isn't much of a fight about these matters. The Church's teaching on sex, gender, and reproduction (better: *procreation*) is seen as just so outdated, obviously wrong, and evil that direct challenges almost never happen.

To the extent that the Church's tradition and teaching are even approached, appeals to experience are the trump cards for making sure an actual argument doesn't break out. "Someone's humanity should never be up for discussion" is now a classic rhetorical move designed to shut down debate and enforce a false orthodoxy. Another favorite is the appeal to the "violence" that these views supposedly produce. Dissenters from contemporary progressive orthodoxy are without options: in whatever direction they move, they will earn a scarlet letter.

It goes without saying that this kind of ideology and methodology are simply incompatible with the name "Catholic." Unlike the approach Professor Rubio has courageously decided to take, this approach is totally missing anything like unity with the Church. A foreign ideology and methodology are running the show.

6. Opportunities for Unity-in-Diversity

Given the massive amount of diversity here—and the yawning chasm between the average progressive Catholic professor and those who, say, consider themselves traditional Catholics—it becomes particularly important to ask what we are willing to sacrifice for the sake of unity. How can we embrace Jesus forsaken and get comfortable with the profound discomfort involved in trying to find unity-in-diversity in this context?

There are opportunities for important exchanges to be had. The ways that progressive Catholic professors offer historical challenges could lead to very important conversations about the development of doctrine, the place of personal conscience, and the role the Holy Spirit has played in guiding the Church through the long and winding roads leading to our present moment. Pope Francis, supported by overwhelming majorities across the Catholic political spectrum, could also be a unifying figure here.[11] On the one hand, he's strongly in favor of prenatal justice, harshly critical of contemporary gender ideology, and focused on the given reality of the human body as a gift reflecting God's creative plan. On the other hand, he's explicitly focused on encounter, welcoming, hospitality, and mercy for those who do not typically feel welcomed by the institutional Church. Pope Francis's personal witness in holding these in balanced tension with each other is, all by itself, a powerful resource for bridge-building.

A focus on the body could also be a place for finding unity-in-diversity. Is it too much to ask to put ideology aside, have a St. Robert Bellarmine–like focus on what the science tells us about our bodies and imitate his willingness to change our minds in light of the evidence? We are not invisible ghosts, after all, but embodied souls. Our bodies, as Christ's Resurrection makes clear, are essential to who we are. They are not ours to manipulate in whatever way we see fit.

Sorry-not-sorry, transhumanists.

But this view also pushes up against some conversations surrounding sex and gender, especially when it comes to children getting hormones and/or surgery in an attempt to transition from a boy to a girl (far more likely) or from a girl to a boy.[12] But as our challenging mentors have reminded us, these kinds of discussions—while they must invoke the best science out there—must also be accompanied by putting the good of the other before our own.

In other words, engagement must be accompanied by self-emptying love that, from beginning to end, never wavers from willing the good of the other.

Unfortunately, however, discussions about issues our brothers and sisters who identify as gay, lesbian, bisexual, trans, and so forth hold dear are far too often darkened by an approach in which the reasoning offered is little more than an *ex post facto* justification for bigotry. Indeed, the fact that these populations get singled out (especially relative to heterosexual populations who habitually use contraception and porn, reproduce children via IVF, divorce and remarry, and so on) sends a very clear, albeit contradictory, message as to what is actually going on here.

The Church needs an all-hands-on-deck effort to do better. To be the first to will the good of the other. To do everything we can to demonstrate that we cherish the humanity of the person in our Catholic family before we can even begin, carefully and thoughtfully, to have a fruitful discussion or a genuine argument. Our challenging mentors can check us in extremely helpful ways as we try to move toward this goal.

Conclusion

A final consideration might be how we can foster a mutual conversation about what it would mean to push back against the ideological excess that currently dominates academia and renew our focus on welcoming a genuinely diverse group of folks into our circle of conversation. A sci-fi convention that would welcome both Star Wars fans and Trekkies, if you will.

Building an intentional culture of encounter across the political and ideological differences mentioned above could reveal substantial and important common ground across many different issues, including working to support women in their desire to have children they feel social pressure to abort.

There's also important overlap and interesting dialogue to be explored when it comes to discussions of race and racism, not least because people of color (and especially immigrants to the United States) tend to be much more religious and much more traditional in their beliefs and practices than is the average progressive Catholic professor.

And this, it turns out, will be a very important consideration for our next chapter.

8

The Immigrant Parent

I.e., "The Leaven Catholic"

1. The Thin Caricature

Let's do a thought experiment to begin. Let's say you are hanging out with a parishioner who has had one beer too many at the annual festival, and he starts complaining about "the Mexicans" in the parish and how they want a special Mass all to themselves in Spanish, separate from the rest of the parish. "Why can't they just learn English?" he asks.

And, then, way too loudly, he goes on: "What's wrong with these immigrants? They fawn all over these people on the news—probably because they clean their houses, raise their kids, and do their yardwork, right? The differences between them and us—us *real* Americans—are actually *celebrated*. The so-called melting pot isn't so melty these days, is it?"

At this point you begin to nervously look away, both to try to find an exit out of the conversation and to make sure no one who might associate you with his views is listening to this guy.

"You do hear what I'm saying, right?" your increasingly hostile interlocutor asks. "It's another attempt to undermine *our* culture. The government and media just ignore the hordes of immigrants who will do nothing but reject American values, have lots of babies, and bring their diseases and socialism with them. They'll drive down working-class wages, get onto welfare, send money back home, and vote for radical Democrats."

You're seconds away from noticing a friend across the parking lot who can pull you away from this disaster of an exchange, but you manage to stay conscious long enough to hear him finish.

"And it would be one thing if it were only these Mexican parishioners asking for special treatment, but have you noticed that more and more priests are immigrants just off the boat themselves? I heard a rumor that we're getting a new priest from Mexico. I guess we need to get ready to not be able to understand his homilies—except, of course, for when he's going on and on about socialism."

Perhaps you didn't have to imagine this scene. Maybe you've experienced something like it.

2. What Is in Our Hearts?

This is an especially important chapter to focus on what is behind a thin caricature that so spectacularly fails to respect even basic human dignity—much less the fact that "the Mexicans" (and the Nigerians, Haitians, Filipinos, Vietnamese, Brazilians, et al.) are our brothers and sisters in Christ. In certain cases—let's face it—the thin caricatures of immigrants we encounter may be grounded in racism. A sense that "real American" Catholics in the United States are white and that nonwhite Catholics just don't belong here, or don't belong in the same way as whites do, is far less common than it used to be, but these heinously insular points of view still exist.

It is difficult to say, however, that racism is the primary driving force here. After all, plenty of white conservative Catholics feel their hearts go aflutter every time they come across a clip of a Latino such as Senator Ted Cruz making a melodramatic speech invoking something like the caricature above. More significant than racism is an idolatrous focus on preserving one's understanding of a national culture and of one's political power too.

It is of course a very old thing to find established populations worried about threats to their culture coming from immigrants. The US Catholic Church—built largely by Italian, Irish, Polish, and German immigrants—should know this better than most, given that we were shunned by the established WASP American culture for the better part of a century. You've seen old photos of the signs, right? "No Irish (Italian, Colored, etc.) Need Apply." The difference in those cases was that the established culture was *not* Catholic and saw the Catholic faith in the "hordes" of immigrants coming into the country as a particular threat.

Today, however, it is often Catholics themselves—now very much part of the established culture—who are shunning Catholic immigrants perceived to be threats to the culture in which we now hold some power. Get this: only fifteen of the 115 total Supreme Court justices who have ever served on the bench have been Catholic. But today six of the nine justices were raised in the Catholic faith. Other than jean jackets coming back in style, this might be the biggest cultural turnaround in recent memory.

Catholic immigrants to this country remind us that our faith is broader and deeper than our dominant US culture and that we should not diminish our identity as Catholics in order to conform to it. Indeed, new Catholic immigrants should remind us that much of that culture is in strong tension with what the Church teaches and some of it is utterly hostile. For US Catholics who are part of the cultural establishment, immigrants can provide an uncomfortable but necessary reminder that many of us are latching onto and benefiting from a deeply problematic culture.

If you are someone who needs a reminder of the good that Catholic immigrants can provide, then it behooves you to listen with humility. I also offer this perspective out of my own experience of marrying into an immigrant Filipino family, which I'll discuss in more detail later. For now, I'll say that joining an immigrant family has made me profoundly grateful to be both challenged and supported by immigrants with a very different set of experiences than my own.

3. A Story That Thickens

Recently, I had an extended exchange with a friend of mine I'll call José. He traveled to mainland United States after finishing college and postgraduate education in Puerto Rico. His future wife, whom I'll call Thania, also moved from Puerto Rico and met José at an Advent retreat for young adults in the mid-1990s.

Though they were both technically US citizens, they did not in any shape or form "feel" American upon their arrival to New England. While they loved many features of American culture and had affection for their neighbors and friends, they were very much cultural immigrants and most often felt like strangers.

José said that he felt as if he had moved to a foreign country. One of his first shocks was a revealing one. Christmas was so overly consumeristic and, in his words, "lame." In contrast to the joy and party atmosphere of the prolonged holiday season in Puerto Rico, the holidays were totally sterile for the "Americanos" he met. He could not understand how, even among many fellow Catholics, the joy he had experienced back home seemed to be missing.

Thania remembered the discrimination she suffered both in school and in the workplace because of her accent and because she was a Latina—even in what was known to be a "progressive" part of the country. She observed that the general American culture could be very oppressive. José added that the established culture seemed intent on erasing the differences brought here by people from other cultures. In a US context, one might think José and Thania were describing people on the political right. This was accurate to a degree. But José and Thania were keen to point out that both wings of American politics were very exclusive. "And Latinos feel it," they said.

As an example of this type of reception coming from the left, José brought up the supposedly inclusive term "Latinx." Noting that the word is completely illogical in the Spanish language, which distinguishes words as feminine or masculine, he said that many of his friends and acquaintances describe this as a push to homogenize Latinos via "another cultural invasion devised by the Anglos."

José and Thania particularly mourn this trend as it has played out in the Church. They are keenly aware of how many US Catholics choose political affiliation over fidelity to faith. Back in the 1980s, a friend of José's in Puerto Rico suggested that US Catholics pretend to "teach Catholicism to the pope" in light of their secular politics. To them, the sense of entitlement among US Catholics was palpable. José suggested this was something derived from a Protestant, individualistic mindset that prevents a true Catholic ethos from flourishing.

True Catholic ethos plays out in ways that are strange in a US political context. José was adamant that the labels *liberal* and *conservative* "have no place within a Catholic identity." Like many Latinos, he and his wife are "conservative" on issues related to family, life, and sexuality. But they insist they are not conservative when it comes to some of the views portrayed in the media. Indeed, they see no contradiction at all with the more "liberal" views they hold on issues of social justice, including a deep desire to welcome and learn from immigrants.

José and Thania both lamented that this countercultural stance is beginning to change only because American culture is swallowing up many Latino cultures. This is especially true for young people, including their own young adult children. Like many of their peers, none of their three children still attend Mass. Instead, "they're living the dominant US culture" and no longer practice Catholicism or any other religion. This, José and Thania said, "has broken our hearts."

One thing they thought stood out in Latino cultures that may differ from other US contexts is the still deep value of family and family ties. Even though their daughters have stopped going to Church, they still maintain a link to Catholicism through their interactions with their parents. "It's a cultural Catholicism, but there is value in that," said José.

4. What Are the Gifts and Truths Being Proclaimed?

First, before jumping into the gifts and truths, it might be a good idea to get a handle on who these folks are.

According to a June 2021 study released by CARA (the standard when it comes statistical analysis of the Church in the United States) based on 2,391 US parishes, about a quarter say they serve at least one immigrant community.[1] The most common communities mentioned were originally from Mexico (328), the Philippines (88), El Salvador (44), and Vietnam (40). Seventy-three sites said they served Hispanic/Latino populations without specifying a country.

More than 21 percent of the parishes indicated that they have at least one Spanish weekend Mass, and 8 percent have a weekend Mass in a language other than English or Spanish. Other than Spanish, the most common languages were Vietnamese, Polish, Portuguese, Korean, Arabic, and Tagalog.

These are powerful reminders of the fact that we are a global Church. They are also deeply inconvenient facts for those who want to identify Catholicism with US culture. Remember, our primary bonds are not as fellow citizens of the United States but as brothers and sisters in Christ. Or at least they should be. Recall St. Paul's insistence that there is no longer "Jew or Greek" but that all are one in Christ Jesus.

Furthermore, moving with hope from one land to another—something that St. Paul knew very well in his own travels, obviously—is an important part of the Christian experience, from its earliest moments right through today.

Catholic immigrants from Europe in the latter half of the nineteenth century were willing to suffer terrible discrimination from an anti-Catholic culture in order to practice their faith. Their way of living—not fully immersed in their new country and not fully forgetful of their old countries—put them in a wonderful position to avoid the idolatry that too often accompanies our cultural status quo.

I've been extremely fortunate to experience this in my own life in my wife's wonderful Filipino family and have seen first-generation immigrants live in this space in between the US and Filipino cultures. Because of this, they are in a much better position than more established populations are to live out their faith—and it shows.

My Filipino relatives have inspired me on numerous occasions to live my faith in important ways when I would otherwise be captured by slothful, self-obsessed US-style individualism. For example, Christmas in our family means a very holy, festive, and full (of food!) celebration of "Simbang Gabi" and a nine-day series of Masses and prayers, fellowship, and meals leading up to Christmas Day. It's easy to resist the mind-numbing consumerism of a typical American Christmas if we are living in the midst of this type of tradition and celebrating it as a tight-knit Catholic community.

This is also true for many Latino communities that have similarly powerful devotional practices, particularly with

Our Lady of Guadalupe, the Day of the Dead, Ash Wednesday, Holy Hour, and more. What an incredible gift Catholic immigrants give to the Church. They convict the comfortable establishment for living in idolatry—while at the same time offering alternatives and resources for resisting it.

5. What Are the Challenges?

Traditional cultural religious practices immigrants bring with them to America are under severe, intense threat. But let's be honest, this isn't any different than what has happened with nonimmigrant populations. We are very familiar with religious elements of a holiday like Christmas being absorbed into secular forms. A crèche may appear alongside Santa Claus and his elf. Among Puerto Ricans, even non-Catholics participate in Good Friday processions, and traditional fish/seafood plates are served every Friday of Lent as an expected tradition.

José and Thania believe that the loss of these cultural practices and cues made it easier for their children to stop practicing their religion. Catholicism was no longer a part of the culture in which they live. This was after José and Thania did what so many Catholic parents before them had done to ensure their children would keep their faith:

- They enrolled their children in a Catholic school, which did help maintain an important connection to the life of the sacraments.

- They made many friends in the Latino Catholic community at their parish, people who to this day have kept reinforcing the faith, especially within a Latino cultural context.

- Their daughters participated in church activities, such as the Christmas pageant and a portrayal of the living

Stations of the Cross, coordinated by members of the parish's Latino community.

- And José and Thania embodied their Catholic faith at every turn at home. But this was still not enough.

A Pew survey from September 2020 supports what happened to this family. The headline of the survey reads: "Hispanic teens enjoy religious activities with parents, but fewer view religion as 'very important.'"[2] Overall, the survey found that Hispanics across all age groups tend to be more religious than Americans overall on several measures, such as regularly attending worship services and saying religion is critical in their lives. The story changes, however, when one looks at younger generations. For instance, the survey also showed that Hispanic teens attend Church services at basically the same rate as US teens overall and that Hispanic teens actually pray before meals with their family less compared to US teens who do so (42 percent to 48 percent).

Given this information, take a look back at the caricature that opened this chapter. The one in which the melting pot isn't so melty when it comes to Catholic immigrants. Turns out it's never been meltier. If anything, US culture is assimilating these and other immigrants quite well—and maybe even faster than ever. But unfortunately, the assimilation is heading in the wrong direction, from traditional religious practices to secular consumerism. Worship events surrounding Simbang Gabi or the Feast of Our Lady of Guadalupe often don't stand a chance against unbridled materialism or an addiction to Instagram or Netflix.

The very basic challenge is that the faith second-generation immigrants have can often be analogized to a First Communion outfit. It may fit them well at eight, but they outgrow it by eighteen. Though there is hostility in the new culture to immigrants, of more danger is that the ideology, economics, and culture of secular America eats it up, and this leads to apathy and disaffiliation for the second-generation immigrant.

This is something we've seen play out already in dramatic ways when it comes to Catholic immigrants from Europe in the nineteenth and twentieth centuries. It is something I've experienced in significant parts of my own Irish and Italian American families.

6. Opportunities for Unity-in-Diversity

A major lesson to learn here, one that has been a consistent idea throughout this book, is that an authentic Catholic faith, one that starts with our common Baptism and commitment to the Gospel as our ultimate source of identity, must do everything it can to avoid an idolatrous acceptance of the values of a surrounding culture that is eating Catholic cultures alive.

This requires creating a robust Catholic counterculture in which we think of ourselves as pilgrims on a journey, never quite at home. It is of course good to love one's country and will the good of its people, to do what we can to make the local and national order better reflect the Gospel. But for Catholics (and all people of faith), it is deeply problematic to make "country" one's highest good. Catholics must get comfortable with being uncomfortable foreigners in a land that is not truly their own.

There is no better reminder of the above truths, and no more powerful example leading us in their direction, than fellow Catholics who are immigrants to our shores. And given some of what we've seen, boy do we need this population to be leaven for our political culture—*post haste*.

The inherent in-between-ness from the old culture to the new has led immigrants and even their children to live—and vote—in ways that are much more resistant to the assumptions and structures of US culture, economics, and ideology. This point cannot be stressed enough. Consider that though votes of immigrants have been taken for granted by the Democratic Party for decades, a recent *Wall Street Journal* poll found that Latino voters are now split evenly between Democrats and Republicans. And this is in spite of some conservatives claiming that Democratic immigration policy is mostly about capturing new voters for themselves.[3]

Also, for decades, Catholics have made up an important vote that could go either way in our presidential elections, with a majority electing the winner nearly every time.[4] But how much more authentic to the Gospel could US Catholics as a group be if we allowed our immigrant communities to move us even more in a politically complex (or even homeless!) direction? What if we truly reflected a Catholic vision on issues of life and family (sometimes called conservative) and a Catholic vision on issues of social justice (sometimes called liberal) in the way many Latino communities do? This would be the height of anti-idolatry, Gospel-centered politics.

For a couple of good examples, I'm thinking of two wonderful Latino bishops who model what this might look like.

Archbishop José Gómez of Los Angeles, a Mexican immigrant, has served many roles within the United States Conference of Catholic Bishops, including, recently, as its president. Earlier he was chairman of the USCCB's committee on migration and wrote a book titled *Immigration and the Next America: Renewing the Soul of Our Nation* in which he called Americans' response to immigrants "the human rights test of our generation."[5] He has had the courage to call out the idolatry of the far left for selling out to a "pseudo-religious" worldview that is hostile to Christianity.[6]

Another clerical example is Bishop Daniel Flores of the Texas border Diocese of Brownsville, which is home to more than one million Catholics. Currently the head of the Committee on Doctrine for the USCCB, Bishop Flores is one of the most publicly committed bishops to proclaiming the Church's authentic teachings in many different areas. But much like Archbishop Gómez, he has the courage to call out the nationalistic idolatry of the right. Indeed, responding to calls to deport immigrants facing murderous threats back in their home countries, Bishop Flores said that such policies entail "brutal" actions that are "not unlike driving someone to an abortion clinic."[7]

Especially after invoking these two beautiful witnesses, I can't help but think about a profound common influence on both of these holy men: their devotion to Our Lady of Guadalupe. Talk about a unity-in-diversity image! She is claimed by the pro-life right as the Patroness of the Unborn (indeed, in her famous image, she is pregnant with the Son of God) in their efforts for prenatal justice. But she is also claimed by the social justice left (for example, the United Farm Workers) as protector of immigrants and other marginalized populations.[8]

This, my friends, is the kind of unity-in-diversity on which authentic Catholic communities can be built.

Conclusion

As José and Thania reminded me, despite the many positive developments for Latinos within the US Church, they often still face an underlying attitude of prejudice and disdain from mainly English-speaking Catholics. There are many Latinos who feel they have to keep proving themselves worthy of sitting at the same table as those who were here as Catholics before them. The decades of prejudice against strangers, as they put it, "sit very tight within a culture," and the strong cultural identity of Latinos doesn't sit well among those who think immigrants should become homogenized and forgetful of the traditions of their homelands.

Against this, we need to build countercultural communities that welcome and even seek out the glorious mix and diversity unified in the Body of Christ, the Church. José and Thania's children are likely facing many of the same issues faced by other young people we've discussed throughout this book, that is, a deep longing for real and embodied community, a willingness to embrace traditional religious practices, and an interest in engaging political complexity.

Remember, the key is building Catholic communities in which disaffected and disaffiliated people come to believe that we see the holy image of God in them. We need to move in concrete ways that demonstrate that we genuinely do care about them.

Having already mentioned my own reversion back to the Catholic faith, I have to say that, though staying even marginally connected to the faith through that of my (Irish and Italian) parents, and still valuing my cultural Catholicism in some sense, it was ultimately joining the communities at both Catholic Memorial High School as a theology teacher and the theology department at the University of Notre Dame as a doctoral student that brought me back to the faith.

All the evidence suggests that, especially for young people—and most especially for young Latinos—we need to build protective, countercultural Catholic communities in which one can be vulnerable, be honest, and, most important, feel at home.[9]

If we can build diverse communities united by our common faith, then there is real hope that children like those raised by José and Thania—unfulfilled, adrift, and even disgusted by an individualist and consumerist US anti-immigrant culture—may join a new generation of Catholic reverts who will lead the US Church into a new and more faithful era.

9

The Christmas and Easter Catholic

I.e., "The Can't Quit Catholic"

1. The Thin Caricature

"What time is midnight Mass?"

I should have given fair warning first: Catholic dad joke alert. Or, at least, parish rectory staff alert. But this chapter's caricature has it on good authority that is an actual question fielded by parish staff on December 24!

What authority, you say? Hmmm. Now that you ask, I'm not sure. But it's the kind of thing the great unwashed who only show up to Mass once or twice a year would ask. You know who I'm talking about, right? The "submarine" Catholics—aka the "CEOs" (Christmas and Easter only) and Chreasters (same)—who surface only on the biggest holidays. Or, if you want something more elegant, the "poinsettia and lily Catholics."

Whatever name we give them, we're talking about those who pack the church so full that we have to get to Mass a full hour early on Christmas so our family can find a seat. Why do these people even show up? Everyone knows they won't be there the next week. Why do they make things so difficult for those of us who are actually Catholic?

I mean, think of the gym on January 2. The regulars who are serious about their health all know that the machines and benches and classes will be full to overflowing with uncommitted people crowding out those of us who are serious about working out. We feel like saying, "Listen, buddy, we all know you won't be here next week, so why don't you get out of my way so I can do some squats?"

Something similar is true of the Christmas and Easter "Catholic." They obviously don't care about what the Church teaches—otherwise, they'd be at Mass far more often. Maybe they feel guilty, but they don't need to cramp our style out of some misplaced sense of the familiar or a vague cultural obligation. We should just give them permission to stay home and leave the space for those of us who are there for serious reasons.

And God forbid we actually engage this crowd about why they only show up once or twice a year. They'll tell you that they "used to be an altar boy" or "went to Catholic school" and that this makes them experts about all things related to the Church, especially since Fr. Smith or Mrs. Jones told them it wasn't a sin to miss Mass and that what really matters is being a good person. Ugh. Sigh. And all the rest.

2. What Is in Our Hearts?

Even if we just skim the gospels, we can't miss the fact that Jesus had no patience for the judgmental purists of his day, that is, those who especially were spewers of contempt at those who weren't great at following religious law. He never said the law wasn't important (see Mt 5:18) but rather that he considered what was in the hearts of the Pharisees and others who wanted to use the law to puff up their egos to be more telling.

Pressed on why he hung out with sinners, Jesus made an analogy to why physicians welcomed and served the sick (see Mk 2:17). The folks whose attitudes of superiority kept those in need of spiritual care from getting access to it received harsh names (like snakes and vipers!) from Jesus (see Mt 23:3). Among Our Lord's most important goals was to find the lost sheep and welcome them back into the fold. And he wasn't going to let self-appointed gatekeepers of the law get in his way.

As mentioned many times in other chapters, we ought to be creating the kinds of communities that can welcome those who have lost their way. The hostile attitude displayed in the gross caricature above does precisely the opposite. Snakes and vipers, indeed!

Furthermore, the focus on our own superiority in relation to others is born of a dangerous illusion.

Peter and Paul, the two most important saints in our tradition, were among the worst sinners around. Paul calls himself this specifically. And Peter—well, what can we say about someone who abandoned and denied Christ multiple times after swearing he would not? Mary Magdalene, the first to see Jesus after his resurrection, had once been possessed by seven demons.

Let's be honest. A good number of those who manage to get themselves to church on Sunday are among the worst at keeping the Sabbath day holy. What room does someone have for talking down to so-called submarine Catholics when, for instance, they spend the rest of the day violating the Third Commandment by selling out to a consumerist and (in a related story) workaholic culture instead of making it a day of rest?

No, for those of us who have something like the caricature above in mind, it is time to ask for both the healing of God's forgiveness and the power of God's sanctifying grace to put self-righteousness aside and welcome and encounter those who are on the margins of the Church.

We can't know what God will do with this, but it could be extraordinary, as the next story reveals.

3. A Story That Thickens

What's the first thing that pops into your head when you hear someone say "Marky Mark and the Funky Bunch"?

If you're under thirty-five, you probably aren't thinking much of anything, except maybe that, whatever it is, it might be just a little bit delicious—especially if you unconsciously added an *r* to the final word. *Mmmm. Funky Brunch.*

But for those of us of a certain age (I was in high school when "Good Vibrations" came out), we think of the US hip-hop group fronted by Mark Wahlberg in the early '90s. Yes, this is the same Mark Wahlberg who starred in the *Transformers* and *Planet of the Apes* movies. He won an Academy Award for his role in *The Departed.* Today, he is one of the most highly sought-after talents in Hollywood.

But even those of us who knew of him before he was a movie star might not know about his background growing up.

Mark Wahlberg is the youngest of nine children in a Catholic family from Dorchester, Massachusetts. He attended Catholic school growing up.[1] But he didn't take his faith that seriously, and by age sixteen, he was getting into some serious trouble. In fact, he was tried as an adult and incarcerated for violent crimes.

"When I heard the jail doors close behind me," said Wahlberg. "I started praying right away." The faith he had abandoned came back to him when he needed it most, and it helped him move in a very different direction.

But even after this episode and the beginnings of his success as an actor, Mark Wahlberg was still lost in many ways, and this was revealed most publicly by the kinds of movies he chose to do.

Boogie Nights is a film that stands out as one that con-
flicts with Catholic standards. Not surprisingly, it was highly acclaimed by Hollywood (indeed, it may have been the
film that put Wahlberg on the map), winning three Academy
Awards, including best original screenplay. But at least part
of the reason it was so acclaimed was because of the way it
engaged the so-called golden age of porn from the 1970s.
While it honestly shows the decline, corruption, and downfall
of porn, the movie ends with Wahlberg's character (a porn
performer at the center of the story) looking at his genitals in
front of a mirror and telling himself: "I am a star."

Wahlberg appears to be in quite a different place today.
In a show of genuine humility, he has even apologized to the
pope for some of his movie choices.[2]

"Being a Catholic is the most important aspect of my
life," says Wahlberg. He wants "to serve God and to be a good
human being and to make up for the mistakes I made and the
pain I put people through."[3] Not only does he try to attend
Mass each day (even when he is on location shooting a film)
but also his daily routine reveals that he begins his day at what
I used to consider the ungodly hour of 2:30 a.m. with prayer.[4]

So, yes, take a good look at what God has done with Marky
Mark. It is difficult to imagine what would have become of
him if priests and other Catholics close to him had dismissed
his return to the Church as unserious and then abandoned
him to go back to a more typical Hollywood lifestyle. Those
who stood by him not only became conduits for God's grace
but also helped Wahlberg himself become such a conduit.
The result is that millions have been inspired by his example.

4. What Are the Gifts and Truths Being Proclaimed?

Not everyone has this kind of dramatic "reversion" to the faith,
and not everyone who does, of course, is a famous Hollywood
actor. Many are people like my own younger brother who was

married in the Church, fell away after his divorce, and went on with his life while God continued to chip away at him over time. After he came to my uncle's funeral and renewed relationships with Catholic extended family, he slowly began his way back to the faith.

Let's explore a bit more about what we know about these Christmas and Easter Catholics.

First, even among those who identify with the faith, Catholics as a whole don't go to Church that often. In fact, according to CARA, only about half of self-identified Catholics attend Mass at least once a month.[5] And according to a recent survey commissioned by The Pillar, 29 percent of self-identified Catholics said they went "never" or "less than once a year."[6]

It has become something of a joke—or at least a quippy "didn't you know" interjection in a social setting—to note that ex-Catholics would be the largest Christian denomination in the United States and even the third-largest religion in the country overall. But as we saw in the chapter on Gen Z "nones," plenty of folks who don't identify with a particular faith still believe in God and still find themselves at church from time to time—especially on Christmas and Easter.

The Pillar survey (done in late 2021—well after churches were back open after being closed during the pandemic) also found quite informative and interesting reasons why people stop going to Mass. Only 14 percent of those surveyed gave a reason that had something to do with faith concerns. "My beliefs about God or religious practice changed" came in as the fifth most important reason for not going to Mass. The top four are more easily correctable:

- I moved away from the church I had been attending. (20 percent)

- I did not feel that attending church mattered. (19 percent)

- I moved away from my family. (17 percent)
- I had a change of circumstances (work, health, family situation) that made it harder to attend. (15 percent)

These results reveal that there aren't truly major obstacles to keep most people from reverting back to the faith. Indeed, even though the Church (with some notable exceptions) doesn't do a great job of reaching out to marginalized or disaffected folks, a fairly high number retain some kind of firm (if amorphous) connection to the Church despite their ups and downs. Time and time again, even as our culture sees lots of religious disaffiliation, we find that Roman Catholicism has the highest retention rate among all denominations and faiths. For example, the numbers of self-identified Catholics held steady (24 to 21 percent) during a fourteen-year period from 2007 to 2021, while Protestants experienced dramatic falls (from 52 percent to 40 percent of the US population) during the same period. Catholic membership has actually increased since 2019.

We might think that these numbers are holding steady due to immigration, but given the significantly lower number of Baptisms, the higher number of deaths, and the relatively low number of adult converts, a significant number of reverts to the Catholic faith must help explain these numbers.[7] Indeed, CARA estimates that there are between 150,000 and 200,000 people who come back to the faith every year in the United States.

Why am I throwing all this data at you? Because it just goes to show that it's very hard to quit being Catholic.

One of the great gifts of Christmas and Easter Catholics is that, perhaps counterintuitively, they demonstrate the power of Christ's Church to stay connected with people, even through their marginalization or disaffection. One of my favorite movie lines is from *Dogma*, when the main character, a thirty-something disaffected Catholic named Bethany, says of her being in church, "I don't know why I keep coming here."

As you've learned, in my early twenties I was very much like Bethany. Even when I was on the verge of rejecting almost everything about the Church, something kept me connected. And that something was God's grace brought about through the sacraments. Throughout my disaffection, I never once stopped being a temple of the Holy Spirit. I was always primed to come back home.

And what amazing gifts those who come back home bring to the family! Though not as well known as Marky Mark, their witness has the power to move many—both inside and outside the Church. This is especially true when they can show that the joy and peace they are so clearly experiencing as a result of their reversion is possible in a culture so dominated by depression and anxiety.

One of the most important sources of these stories is *The Journey Home* show on EWTN as part of the Coming Home Network. Record numbers (hovering around 5,000) of reversions or conversions per year are supported by this ministry.[8] Most of the stories (which include video interviews on their website) are just about regular folks, and I encourage you to watch them.[9] If you have any sense that the Church is somehow dead or that the Holy Spirit has left us, these moving stories will slap that kind of defeatism right upside the head.

But the story with which I'd like to finish this section on the gifts is about twenty-one-year-old Omar Lopez. He was a young man who, "feeling pretty lost himself," went to hear Mark Wahlberg talk at an event for young adults put on by the Archdiocese of Chicago and then returned to the Church.[10] Isn't it amazing how connected the Church is? Those who never gave up on a CEO Catholic like Marky Mark indirectly helped bring a young, Latino "none" back into the fold. The mutually reinforcing ways in which we can build a counter-cultural Catholic community are there for the taking.

5. What Are the Challenges?

What if I told you that if you went to the public library and listened to an hour-long audio lecture for only one day a week, $50,000 would immediately appear in your bank account? And if you did it again the next week, the same thing would happen? How hard would it be for me to get you there?

I'm going to guess it wouldn't be that hard. Indeed, even if this was a completely solitary and lonely experience, people would still be crawling all over each other to be able to reserve a space for the lecture.

Next, think about being able to be a part of the Holy Sacrifice of the Mass, to commune with God himself, to have his Body become one with yours, and to get a foretaste of heaven. Those kinds of rewards put $50,000 to shame. The Eucharist is as good as it gets for us here on Earth. The Eucharist, the Second Vatican Council taught, "is the source and summit of the Christian life."

Why wouldn't people show up for Sunday Mass? The only way this makes sense is if they don't know or actually believe that the Real Presence of Christ is in the Eucharist. Well, it turns out that a 2019 Pew poll gave Catholics the choice between (A) the bread and wine used during Communion are symbols of the Body and Blood of Christ and (B) the bread and wine actually become the Body and Blood of Christ, and 69 percent of the respondents answered A. Only 31 percent answered B.[11]

I found these to be astonishing, heartbreaking numbers. But they do help explain why a relatively high number don't go to Mass. It's because they don't see why it matters. Why would anyone make an effort to get out of bed, get dressed, and drive to a church for just symbols? Anyone can set up symbols of

Christ's Body and Blood in one's closet or kitchen. If this is how many Catholics view it, I can certainly understand why they have drifted away from Mass.

And though we don't have full data on this yet, it's almost certainly the case that the COVID-19 pandemic has made this already bad problem even worse. Though many of us missed going to Mass and went back as soon as we could, others who were regularly attending have likely had the opposite experience and have remained away.

6. Opportunities for Unity-in-Diversity

The pews in Catholic churches should be full of an incredible diversity of folks. Remember: "Here comes everybody!" This invitation is for not just when it comes to different generations and races, different musical and liturgical preferences but also when it comes to levels of connection and commitment to the faith.

For some, that may mean getting comfortable with being uncomfortable. It may mean worshipping with people who don't have it all figured out or even who hold views we find obviously wrong or even offensive. But this is what being the first to love requires of us. This is what it means to embrace Jesus forsaken. Coming to our Catholic family's table of the Lord means being *with those he has invited to be there*, not necessarily the ones with whom we are the most comfortable.

There has to be give and take as well. All are welcome at the table, but Christ's Church has no authority to reject principles inspired by sacred scripture and sacred tradition. The Eucharist is not a prize for the perfect. If it were, then none of us could receive Communion! But St. Paul reminds us that one is not to take the Body and Blood of Christ in an unworthy manner, which means one needs to not be in a state of mortal sin. Read: *get your butt to Confession first*!

The requirement to be free from mortal sin makes so little sense to many people who aren't formed in the faith, and some view it as an exclusionary hoop to jump through rather than an invitation to get himself or herself right with God. Happily, in July of 2022, the US Church started a massive campaign aimed at a eucharistic revival that, one hopes, will bring hundreds of thousands of people (if not more!) to an understanding of and a relationship with the source and summit of the Christian life.

Are you skeptical about the possibility of such a change? Well, think about this: most of the 69 percent of Catholics who think that the bread and wine are mere symbols *actually thought that this is what the Church teaches.* Maybe the biggest problem we have is that Catholics simply have not been accurately taught about the gifts Christ's Church has to offer. If so, that is a problem that is fairly easy to correct.

Conclusion

So how should we respond if someone asks us a question like "What time is midnight Mass?" Assuming that it isn't a dad looking for laughs or confusion about whether or not the parish is actually having a midnight Mass, we should be doing everything we can to encourage and welcome this person into our midst. (And maybe throw some confession times their way, too!)

And not just at that one Mass.

Recall that the number one and number three reasons people stop attending Mass is simply because they moved away from their previous church or from their family. Like my brother, like Marky Mark, like me, and like so many of those profiled by the Coming Home Network—we are all temples of the Holy Spirit, primed to come home!

We need to be the kinds of people and create the kinds of parish communities that welcome this very large group of people home. And that means treating them like family. I could state that even more precisely: we need to treat them as the family they already are.

And while it is often a relationship between laypeople that leads to this kind of welcoming back into the fold, sometimes it is a relationship with a priest who takes the lead in building and maintaining the person's return. Unfortunately, at least in some circumstances, the avenues for developing relationships between priests and lay folk seem closed off.

10

The Seemingly Standoffish Parish Priest

I.e., "The Solitary Servant"

1. The Thin Caricature

At last we can *finally* lead with something different kinds of US Catholics have in common: complaining about their local parish priest!

In truth, this common complaint isn't exactly unifying, I guess. In fact, the complaints often reflect many of the deep divisions in the US Church we've already engaged: He's too liberal. He's too conservative. He's too masculine. He's too effeminate. He's too old. He's too young. He's a foreigner. He's a spirit-of-Vatican-II priest. He wants the choir to sing in Latin. He's too authoritarian. He never enforces Church teaching. He always talks about abortion. He never talks about abortion. He loves Pope Francis. He hates Pope Francis. He's always asking us for money. He can't raise money to save his life. He's a Marvel guy. He's a DC guy.

But maybe there is one complaint that transcends our divisions. It's that Father just isn't around, and when he is, he's difficult to talk to. All we get is that handshake after Mass or maybe a few polite words at the annual church festival. There's no hope for even a ten-minute conversation with him, much less an actual relationship with someone who is supposed to be shepherding me and my family into a deeper relationship with Christ.

Oh, sure, maybe he has personal relationships with the "in" crowd, a small group of donors and others who are influential in the parish. But for the rank and file in the pews, all he has for us, frankly, is a standoffish attitude that screams, "Don't get close to me" or "I don't have time for you." Most Catholic parishioners probably have a closer relationship with their Amazon delivery driver than with their parish priest.

And one more thing: where is the joy in this man? Isn't living out the Gospel supposed to bring us joy? Most of the times we encounter him, he seems miserable and defeated. So we just shake his hand politely, maybe call him up when we need a kid baptized or when a family member dies, but that's as close as we're likely to get.

2. What Is in Our Hearts?

Here is one of the times I won't be too judgmental about what's going on in the hearts of those who have the caricature described in this chapter. It is true that there's a certain subset of Catholics who have an anti-clerical, anti-authority bent in general that may bias them unreasonably against priests. They have a more Protestant attitude, quite common in the United States, which thinks of the Church as a kind of democratic institution in which, at any given time, the views of 50 percent-plus-one of the people is where the power should lie. (This is a disturbing proposition given that 51 percent apparently have a favorable opinion of LeBron James.[1]) They imagine their own inclinations and wills as the primary arbiter of truth—with the tradition and authority of the Church playing no role at all except, of course, as an obstacle to acting on their own inclinations and will.

Admittedly there are plenty of Catholics who hold the same complaints against priests yet are quite deferential to Church authority in general and to clergy in particular. Indeed, part of the reason for wanting a deeper relationship with their pastor in such cases is precisely because they know that relying on their own inclinations and wills to determine what is right and true stinks. And they want guidance from outside of themselves about how they can stink less.

The problem here is that most people haven't the foggiest idea about what's going on in the actual lives of real-life priests. Now of course, like everyone else, priests have different personalities, perspectives, and predilections. (Sorry, my three-year-old son Thaddeus is watching The Letter P episode of *Sesame Street* on a loop these days.) There are certain common sets of misconceptions and concerns about priests, some of which will be illustrated, and perhaps debunked, in the story that follows, but maybe not in the way you might expect.

3. A Story That Thickens

Fr. Josh Whitfield comes out of what one might call a "conservative" background. He converted to Catholicism and left the Episcopal Church because he "felt called to the traditionalism and obedience of Catholicism."[2] Interestingly, he was an ordained Episcopalian priest when he converted and already had a wife and children. According to Church teaching and Jesus's command that no man separate what God has joined, a new Catholic doesn't give up his wife and family in such situations, or his priesthood.

As a traditional Catholic he's not interested in challenging Church teaching and sees his situation as the exception it is. When pressed by a news reporter on changing the teaching on married priests in light of his own situation, Fr. Josh pushed back politely but firmly: "It's people like you who are interested in married priests. Here at St. Rita we just get on with it.

My job is just to do the tasks the bishop has given me as best I can, and try and make it work."

Fr. Josh and others like him find themselves in an odd situation. They converted because they found themselves in love with Christ's Church and its teachings, but they are often embraced by progressive Catholics who want those teachings changed. Fr. Josh admits that it may be more difficult if those like the reporter who questioned him think mostly from common, worldly perspectives. "That's sort of the irritating beauty of Catholicism," he says, "The Church persistently thinks theologically, and not sociologically and not politically, at her best."

Fr. Josh, like many priests, has an insane set of responsibilities. He told me that being a Catholic parish priest "can be the most exhausting ministry in Christendom" and joked that being an Episcopal priest "was the best part-time job I ever had."

Nowadays, Fr. Josh gets up at 4 a.m. to pray and have his morning coffee before he says the early Mass. The week I spoke with him, in addition to prepping and celebrating Sunday Masses and daily Masses, he ministered at the parish school, attended two school Christmas programs and a parish concert of Handel's *Messiah*, visited and anointed six people, officiated two funerals, spent more than ten hours in the confessional, attended four staff meetings, blessed an engaged couple, and more.

Before you think we are dealing with some kind of superhuman here, Fr. Josh also made it clear that priests like him "drop the ball, and spectacularly sometimes" and that he finds that depressing. In reality, some people just slip through the cracks for one reason or another, mostly because parish ministry can be a fire drill, and the priest has to triage his ministry commitments. Or sometimes he just gets tied up or forgets.

Fr. Josh wishes people knew how much parish priests work and how much they should pray for more vocations and for parish priests. He wants us to know that parish priests could use more help from parishioners. Where? "Everywhere," he said. Catholics need to see their parishes "more as communities and less as sacrament distribution centers, like sacramental Walmarts."

He insisted that there is "such glory" in being an usher, a eucharistic minister, a CCD teacher, a reader, or part of groups like the St. Vincent de Paul Society. He wants more Catholics to attend Mass on holy days of obligation, yes, but also to respond to what he called "holy services of obligation."

The points Fr. Josh makes on volunteerism apply to most Catholic parishes. To improve in this area, he says, requires an ecclesial culture that truly cherishes lay ministry and lay leadership. If the priest can't visit a person, for instance, it's not a "second-best" option if a deacon or trained layperson visits. Of course, there are sacramental limitations, he reminds us, but we should be clear that Christ is present in the sister or brother who visits and prays as well. "We need people to step forward to offer themselves."

In Fr. Josh's life, another limitation on his time comes from being a husband and a father. And this, of course, is one of the classic arguments made against normalizing married Catholic priests. But there is a deep grace amid the chaos of balancing all that he has going on, and it is clear that the life-giving aspect of his family, his closest community, actually provides an important source of energy and support for his priestly ministry.

Indeed, as a close observer of the celibate priesthood, he sees quite clearly how loneliness is a deep problem for other parish priests. Even in the increasingly rare situation when priests live in community with other priests, they very often do not share a common life and are essentially isolated bachelors walled off in their own individual existence. Also, the abuse crisis has meant that rectories have become social and domestic no-man's-lands for inviting outsiders inside for dinner or other social gatherings. Basically, all priests are left with are TV, the internet, books, and loneliness. It isn't hard to imagine that such loneliness is a major factor in what he suggests "may be a massive unnoticed mental health crisis."

When Fr. Josh comes home, he's "forced to be normal" by his kids and wife, and that's good for his mental health. "If I had to go back to a lonely rectory or one with a few guys I may or may not like, holed up in my room," he said, "I don't know if I'd make it."

4. What Are the Gifts and Truths Being Proclaimed?

For those who have some of the anti-clerical, anti-authority bent I mentioned above, here's an opportunity to be the first to love and listen to the stories of priests with humility. When you put away the Protestant impulse to imagine your own individual inclinations and will as dominant over the authority structures, you will see the incredible gifts these solitary servants offer the Church.

And the solitary part, though in some ways problematic, is an essential part of what multiplies these gifts. While rare married priests like Fr. Josh are staying home to take care of a family sick with the flu, another priest without a family is free to hear confessions, have exchanges with students in religion classes at the parish elementary school, get up in the middle of the night to give last rites and final Communion to a parishioner, and console the deceased person's family.

As one priest I talked to put it, becoming a priest means that Christ's call is his life's priority. His experience of *giving up everything* to follow Jesus allows him to live for God and his Church alone. It is difficult to imagine a more dramatic gift to the Church than this!

This same priest also admitted to me that he never really wanted to become a priest. He and many others who become priests were typically looking for relatively normal lives of marriage, family life, and career just like that of most of their parishioners. Their acceptance of the Sacrament of Holy Orders wasn't an attempt to lord power over anyone, and it certainly wasn't to have a life of self-sacrifice in order to renounce real goods as significant as marriage and family.

Priests are simply called by God and are the rare ones who answer, "Here I am, Lord; I come to do your will."

5. What Are the Challenges?

Picking up on the end of Fr. Josh's story—and regardless of any advantages—the solitary aspect of the solitary servant is a real challenge. One priest I talked with said that being constantly on call is a real challenge as a pastor, especially when his need for rest is crowded out by the relentless responsibilities of his ministry. This has gotten worse over time as more and more parishes have only one priest or one priest is pastor for a merged parish with two or more communities as his responsibility.

Those types of situations often leave priests without the time or inclination to form real relationships, even though, like everyone, they need close relationships to help them process what they go through on a weekly and even daily basis. They are around people all the time, yet their schedule is not their own, so downtime is often spent alone.

Case in point: during the Christmas season, Fr. Conor McDonough, OP, tweeted out the following:

> Being ordained a priest changed Christmas for me completely. Priestly ministry puts me in constant

contact with people who are suffering, and that suffering is often intensified at Christmas. It's a time when I become more aware of the darkness that many people face. This year I'm thinking of a couple whose daughter is in a coma after a brain injury, the wife of a man who has been intubated for six weeks, and the homeless woman who will give me a present, as she always does, because there's no one else to whom she can give a present.[3]

If these kinds of realities can overcome the joy of Christmas, even for a man so connected to the meaning of this great feast, it is simply impossible for many of us to imagine the unending suffering that priests enter into as they serve the Church. This type of suffering occurs not just at Christmas, obviously, but throughout the entire year and is mostly experienced alone.

Priestly morale is often quite low, with a recent CARA study finding that 20 percent of priests are "dissatisfied" with their lives and 13 percent are "very dissatisfied."[4] There are multiple reasons for this, of course—but, again, loneliness and lack of real, meaningful relationships and community is a major part of the problem.

Why don't priests have more and better relationships with their parishioners? Fr. Josh said that at least part of the story is the kind of clericalism that leads to idolization of priests. This often serves as a buffer, quarantining priests apart from the faithful, with everyone stunted in pious unreality. Priests get used to it and hide behind it because it keeps them at a safe distance. Laypeople like it because it funds a devotion that can sometimes deflect from the challenge of holiness. "If I praise the priest," they think, "that may offset my own failures as a disciple."

Another problem is that, as well as not seeing their pastor as part of their circle of relationships, parishioners don't see the entire parish community that way either. One priest

I spoke with said that he liked being invited to events such as Baptism and First Communion parties but that even before the pandemic, he noticed he was receiving fewer and fewer invitations to people's homes. The sex abuse crisis has, again, undoubtedly played a role here. And the hesitation of many priests to connect to others may come from insecurity related to that. Indeed, many priests now approach interactions where they are introduced as a priest expecting to be distrusted.[5]

With that as an expectation, it is difficult to get a real relationship off the ground.

6. Opportunities for Unity-in-Diversity

We definitely need a different model of relationship between priests and the lay faithful. Honestly, the Church may not have a choice. Fr. Thomas Berg argues that bare demographic facts will necessitate a major shift, especially given that "the number of active priests in ministry will continue to decrease due to death, retirement, and an attrition rate among able-bodied priests who abandon the ministry for different reasons." Especially in the Northeast and Midwest, "most dioceses are going to be forced into a strategic reorganization of parish life."[6]

One of the hopeful aspects of this reorganization, suggests Fr. Berg, is that a greater number of priests will be living communally and serving a dramatically reduced number of parishes, thus opening the door for the kind of intentional communal life priests so desperately need.

But the shift is also going to arise, according to Berg, because newly ordained priests will be "subjected to unrealistic and impossible demands on their time, being made by pastors of parishes—often multiple parishes—far too soon and leaving them feeling simply overwhelmed by the responsibilities and demands placed on them." This possibility necessitates a very different relationship between priests and laypeople. One that imagines a new way of doing unity-in-diversity.

Fortunately, a solution is staring us right in the face, points out John Cavadini in a masterful piece for *Church Life Journal* titled "Co-Responsibility: An Antidote to Clericalizing the Laity?" He says the documents of Vatican II, Pope Benedict XVI, and Pope Francis have advocated for a new direction that finally implements the council's vision of two priesthoods—a ministerial priesthood based on ordination and a common priesthood rooted in Baptism.[7]

Lumen Gentium states:

> Though they differ from one another in essence and not merely in degree, the common priesthood of the faithful and the ministerial or hierarchical priesthood are nonetheless interrelated: each of them in its own special way is a participation in the one priesthood of Christ. The ministerial priest, by the sacred power he enjoys, teaches and rules the priestly people; acting in the person of Christ, he makes present the Eucharistic sacrifice, and offers it to God in the name of all the people. But the faithful, in virtue of their royal priesthood, join in the offering of the Eucharist. They likewise exercise that priesthood by receiving the sacraments, by prayer and thanksgiving, by the witness of a holy life, and by self-denial and active charity. (10)

Cavadini emphasizes that the "baptismal priesthood of all the faithful" means that we are all called to make the spiritual sacrifice of taking up a significant role of ministry in the Church. It was building on this foundation that Pope Benedict said that the Church "needs a change of mindset particularly concerning lay people. They must no longer be seen as collaborators of the clergy, but truly recognized as 'co-responsible' for the Church's being and action."[8]

Pope Francis built on Benedict's words by emphasizing the "responsibility of the laity, grounded in their Baptism and Confirmation" that should lead the Church to count on their "deeply-rooted sense of community and great fidelity to the tasks of charity, catechesis and the celebration of the faith." He also refers to Benedict's "change in mindset" by lamenting that lay coresponsibility has been uneven due to both a lack of formation and "an excessive clericalism which keeps them away from decision-making. (*Evangelii Gaudium* 102).

There is a leadership role as head and shepherd for those who receive the gift of the priesthood through the Sacrament of Holy Orders, no question. But the baptismal priesthood of all the faithful, all those who make up the Church as the mystical Body of Christ, share in no sense a "lesser priesthood." All have their essential role to play in preaching and living the Gospel.

Returning to Cavadini's central point, since Vatican II, we've thought about lay participation and responsibility in terms of power, that is, keeping the same "excessively clerical-ized" and "secular" top-down structure in place. A vision of Church in which coresponsible leadership of the priesthood of the baptized was the norm, says Cavadini, hasn't really been imagined yet. Such a vision wouldn't "displace or render irrel-evant the hierarchy or its leadership," but would find the fruits of that leadership precisely in the leadership of the baptized in their own proper sphere.

The key is to find a unity-in-diversity that makes such coresponsibility possible. And that takes the creation of com-munity and a mutual willingness to accept and receive help and instruction.

Conclusion

You may be thinking something like the following: "OK, Camo-sy, this all sounds well and good, but implementing the kind of vision that Vatican II, Benedict, Francis, and Cavadini have in mind here will take a massive institutional shift in the Church—especially from our bishops. What can *we* do about it?"

Sure, it will ultimately require the buy-in of those who formally lead and shape our institutions. (Though keep in mind, again, that demographics may force their hand.) Still, very clear steps can be taken *right now* on the local levels of the Church. These steps could lead to the kinds of relationships that could then lead to the kind of coresponsibility laypeople must have in the Church—while freeing priests up to do more of the kind of ministry proper to their particular role in the Body of Christ as well.

One priest I talked with came to the priesthood after a career in business, and despite this background, it was clear that he could still use help in a number of finance and management-related areas at his parish. And if that's the case for him, can you imagine what priests without this background are facing? From HR to HVAC, our local parish priest needs our help.

So many of us are so busy with our own jobs and families that it may seem difficult to imagine how we could find the time to contribute, yet most of us manage to find the time for the things that really matter to us. For many of us, there are loads of significant time currently going to Instagram, Netflix, and YouTube that could really go to the Church. (Don't believe me? Check the breakdown of app usage on your phone if you dare.)

Another priest I talked to made a point of sharing how much he really enjoyed being around what he called "the family ecosystem," that is, multiple generations of parents, grandparents, and children. (I might add dogs and other pets here; I wish more priests had animal companions!) So, again, it could be as simple as inviting your parish priest to family parties and events—even parties and events unrelated to church! Additionally, and more intentionally, it would be wonderful to forge small communities of often isolated and lonely retired laypeople with often isolated and lonely priests.

For many laypeople, all of this may seem like a heavy lift, especially when faced with someone who, at least on the surface, is, well, a standoffish priest. But I can't tell you how many priests I've talked to, and know personally, who are introverts by nature and don't easily form these kinds of relationships. And, remember, they are also very overworked.

The consistent advice I got from priests was to "let relationships happen naturally" by just showing up. Go to Mass regularly. Sign up for parish offerings. Serve. Help. Do life together.

Fr. Josh reminded me that, like any friendship, it cannot be forced.

It might seem odd to think of the relationship with a priest as one of friendship, especially if one has the kind of problematic clericalism in mind that we've discussed. But remember that the kind of relationship Christ called his followers to was one of friendship, not master and servant. He explicitly said, "I call you friends." The kind of relationship that Jesus wants us to forge with one another is that of an intimate friendship.

If the King of kings and Lord of lords can see our relationship as one of friendship, then what are *we* waiting for? Turn off Netflix, and go to Mass. Determine what your parish community—your Catholic family—needs from you, and then do it!

Part IV

GETTING "THERE" FROM "HERE"

Conclusion

That All May Be One

As the secular culture frays around us, we must ask ourselves: "What is this thing that binds us all together?" The answers are less than clear, especially as more and more of us define ourselves primarily by opposition to large numbers of our fellow citizens. (And, yes, I do have to work on my attitude toward Cardinals fans.)

These antagonistic identities make it difficult to have national conversations, much less debates, about anything of importance. For, as political commentator David French puts it, "When you argue politics with a person, you're often not simply asking them to change their mind, you're often asking them to change their identity. You're asking them to possibly lose their community and forfeit friendships. You're sometimes asking them to shift the very sense of purpose that has defined their life."[1]

But this is not how it should work for our Catholic family. Our diversity of views and approaches should not lead us to define ourselves by opposition to each other. Instead, we should understand that our identity comes from our relationship with God in Jesus Christ, as well as with other Catholics who make up different parts of the mystical Body of Christ into which we have all been baptized. Our disagreements with each other do not risk our primary and ultimate identity as one Catholic family.

The Focolare Movement was born when its founders opened the scriptures to Jesus's prayer that all his followers may be one—in the way that Jesus and the Father are one (Jn 17:21). I mentioned in the introduction that I'm a fanboy of the Focolare Movement, and I want everyone to know just how important this approach to difference within the Church is for us right now. We must embrace our differences with a warm curiosity, knowing that we are united as a Church not in spite of our diversity but *because* of it.

The very notion of relationship requires difference! The unity-in-diversity of the Church is meant to imitate the unity-in-diversity of the Trinity itself.

Focolare followers understand that, for human beings, getting to this kind of unity can be *incredibly* difficult. In working toward this goal, we must embrace the call to humility, to making ourselves small in the presence of the other. At times, it will ask us to embrace the pain of Jesus forsaken. This is not papering over our real differences with happy talk. This can't be the way we think in a Church where Paul told off Peter to his face.

Healthy families still have fights—sometimes really bad fights. But healthy families rest in the security of knowing that they remain family throughout it all and that those bonds will not be broken. So it should be with our Catholic family.

As I was writing this book, I often thought about the US Catholic generation inhabited by my great-grandparents. For them, there was simply no other way to be: their Catholic faith ran the show. Though I didn't understand why she asked me at the time, my great-grandma Mary's only question to me after meeting my first girlfriend was "Is she Catholic?"

Is it possible for US Catholics to recapture the sense that being Catholic is the most essential part of who we are? This goal should be in the hearts of all of us as we pray because

God's grace will certainly be necessary for helping to bring it about.

But I also think about the on-the-ground realities in the United States and feel hopeful. We've seen how Catholic immigrants, especially, help remind us of our primary loyalties. The collapse of US secular political parties and other major institutions, the slouch toward virtual reality and the "metaverse," and the COVID-19 pandemic have all led to unprecedented numbers of people searching for real communities that can give their lives meaning.

Rather than being mere vending machines for the sacraments, Catholic parishes need to step up and become those real communities of genuine, embodied encounter across difference with others and especially with Jesus Christ in person, in the flesh of the Holy Eucharist. After all, the closer we get to Christ, the closer we get to each other.

It is also up to many (*most? something close to all?*) of us to attend our territorial parish—the parish of our actual embodied, local community—and not just go "parish shopping" to have our individualistic needs met. Among other things, that risks replicating our isolated bubble, containing only folks who think pretty much as we do.

Sure, in our current cultural and political moment, it won't be easy to work on encounters with people who think so differently than we do. But never forget Jesus forsaken. If we aren't willing to embrace him, then we simply aren't going to achieve unity-in-diversity.

This book has been written in advance of the 2022 national midterm elections in the United States and will be read (I hope!) in the two years leading up to the next presidential election. If recent history is any guide, the next two to three years are going to be very difficult ones for large communities of people with substantial political and ideological differences. The Catholic Church is definitely included.

We must be as clear as we can be that though civil authority plays an important role in our lives (and especially the lives of the most vulnerable), it is not our ultimate authority and certainly nothing like our ultimate concern.

Though it can be good to participate in the political process and work to achieve just political ends, that is only so if we intentionally put what is going on into perspective and refuse to make an idol of the process or the results. We must always see our fellow Catholics as members of our family first and secular political opponents second.

Different, but the same.

For US Catholics to move toward the goal of being united in our diversity, we need to make progress on several knotty problems that—let's be honest—don't seem to have super clear solutions. We will need the Holy Spirit to do something new in us. No frivolous happy talk here!

In the face of such challenges, let us ask for the intercession our Blessed Mother. And let us invoke, in particular, Our Lady, Undoer of Knots.[2] Devotion to her has exploded in many places all over the world in the last three decades or so, and she has a special place in the spiritual life of our Holy Father, Pope Francis.[3] The devotion's history goes all the way back to St. Irenaeus of Lyons, Doctor of Unity, and his *Against Heresies,* in which he writes that the knot of Eve's disobedience was loosed by Mary.

Let us ask our Blessed Mother to join in the prayer of her Son that all may be one.

Mary, Undoer of Knots, *pray for us.*

Notes

Introduction

1. Katherine Stewart, "How Big Money Is Dividing American Catholicism," The New Republic, March 9, 2021, https://newrepublic.com/article/161626/big-money-dividing-american-catholicism.

2. Bill Bishop, *The Big Sort: Why the Clustering of Like-Minded American Is Tearing Us Apart* (Boston: Mariner Books, 2009).

3. The Focolare Movement (or the "The Work of Mary") is a lay apostolate of the Catholic Church first formed before the hearth (*focolare* in Italian) of a group of Italians during the Allied bombing of Trent in 1943. They first opened the scriptures together to Jesus's prayer to the Father "that all may be one" and since that time have spread their message of Trinitarian unity and dialogue to 180 nations. For more, see "History," Focolare Movement, accessed July 12, 2022, https://www.focolare.org/en/movimento-dei-focolari/storia/.

4. Astute readers will note that I am Gen X and that there is no explicit chapter for Gen X. The simple reason for this is that Gen X, as its name implies, doesn't really have a reputation in these debates! Except, maybe, a reputation for having no reputation. But that was far too meta to be the basis of a chapter for this book.

1. Getting to Unity-in-Diversity

1. Charles C. Camosy, "The Focolare Have Two Words for Our Broken Political Dialogue: Jesus Forsaken," Religion News Service, January 31, 2020, https://religionnews.com/2020/01/31/the-focolare-have-two-words-for-our-broken-political-dialogue-jesus-forsaken/.

2. Courtney Mares, "Pope Francis: 'The Beatitudes Always Bring Joy,'" Catholic News Agency, January 29, 2020, https://www.catholicnewsagency.com/news/pope-francis-the-beatitudes-always-bring-joy-13335.

3. Sabrina Tavernise, "These Americans Are Done with Politics," *New York Times*, November 17, 2018, https://www.nytimes.com/2018/11/17/sunday-review/elections-partisanship-exhausted-majority.html.

2. The Spirit-of-Vatican-II Boomer

1. Peter Wolfgang, "The Failings and the Surprising Virtues of the Vatican II Priests," *Catholic Herald*, April 12, 2021, https://catholicherald.co.uk/the-failings-and-the-surprising-virtues-of-the-vatican-ii-priests/.

2. John Cavadini, "Was Vatican II a Bad Seed?" *Church Life Journal*, July 29, 2020, https://churchlifejournal.nd.edu/articles/is-vatican-ii-bad-seed/.

3. Stephen Bullivant, *Mass Exodus: Catholic Disaffiliation in Britain and America since Vatican II* (Oxford: Oxford University Press, 2019).

4. Claude Sitton, "3 Racists Excommunicated by Louisiana Archbishop," *New York Times*, April 17, 1962, https://www.nytimes.com/1962/04/17/archives/3-racists-excommunicated-by-louisiana-archbishop-perez-mrs-gaillot.html.

5. JD Flynn, "Analysis: As Archbishop Viganò Denounces Vatican II, the Vatican Is Not Speaking," Catholic News Agency, July 1, 2020, https://www.catholicnewsagency.com/

news/45042/analysis-as-archbishop-vigano-denounces-vatican-ii-the-vatican-is-not-speaking.

6. Gerard O'Connell, "Pope Francis Says with Magisterial Authority: The Vatican II Liturgical Reform Is 'Irreversible,'" *America*, August 24, 2017, https://www.americamagazine.org/faith/2017/08/24/pope-francis-says-magisterial-authority-vatican-ii-liturgical-reform-irreversible.

7. Gregory Caridi, "How to Correct Bishops Correctly," *Church Life Journal*, June 3, 2021, https://churchlifejournal. nd.edu/articles/how-to-correct-bishops-correctly/.

3. The Trad Millennial

1. Massimo Faggioli, "A Wake-Up Call to Liberal Theologians," *Commonweal*, May 16, 2018, https://www.commonwealmagazine.org/wake-call-liberal-theologians.

2. Michael Sean Winters, "On the Latin Mass, Pope Francis Pulls Off the Band-Aid," *National Catholic Reporter*, July 16, 2021, https://www.ncronline.org/news/opinion/distinctly-catholic/latin-mass-pope-francis-pulls-band-aid.

3. Stephen G. Adubato, blog, https://www.patheos.com/blogs/cracksinpomo/.

4. Scott Pelley, "The Resurrection of St. Benedict's," *CBS News*, June 26, 2016, https://www.cbsnews.com/news/60-minutes-newark-school-st-benedicts-scott-pelley-2/.

5. Stephen G. Adubato, "Confessions of a 'Weird Catholic,'" *National Catholic Reporter*, June 5, 2020, https://www.ncronline.org/news/opinion/confessions-weird-catholic.

6. Rachel Lu, "Many Catholics Who Felt Lost after Vatican II Found Comfort in the Latin Mass. Now, They Are Hurting Again," *America*, July 21, 2021, https://www.americamagazine.org/faith/2021/07/21/latin-mass-vatican-ii-pope-francis-241093.

7. Peter Feuerherd, "Eucharistic Adoration Is Making a Comeback among Young Catholics," *America*, June 4,

2021, https://www.americamagazine.org/faith/2021/06/04/
eucharistic-adoration-young-catholics-faith-jesus-240798.

8. Michael Brendan Dougherty, "Pope Francis Is Tearing the Catholic Church Apart," *New York Times*, August 12, 2021, https://www.nytimes.com/2021/08/12/opinion/pope-francis-latin-mass.html?smid=tw-share.

9. Steve Adubato, Twitter post, July 17, 2021, 10:59 PM, https://twitter.com/stephengadubato/status/1416593363894218753.

10. Sarah Sparks, "As a Deaf Catholic, the Latin Mass Gives Me Equal Access to the Liturgy," *America*, July 20, 2021, https://www.americamagazine.org/faith/2021/07/20/latin-mass-deaf-catholic-access-liturgy-241084; and Laura Lautaret, Twitter post, July 21, 2021, 8:58 AM, https://twitter.com/LauraLautaret/status/1417831271082954755?s=19.

4. The Gen Z "None"

1. "Brain-Dead Teen, Only Capable of Rolling Eyes and Texting, to Be Euthanized," *The Onion*, January 13, 2012, https://www.theonion.com/brain-dead-teen-only-capable-of-rolling-eyes-and-texti-1819595151.

2. Michael Lipka, "A Closer Look at America's Rapidly Growing Religious 'Nones,'" Pew Research Center, May 13, 2015, https://www.pewresearch.org/fact-tank/2015/05/13/a-closer-look-at-americas-rapidly-growing-religious-nones/.

3. Christian Smith, with Melinda Lundquist Denton, *Soul Searching: The Religious and Spiritual Lives of American Teenagers* (Oxford: Oxford University Press, 2005).

4. Chloé S. Valdary, Twitter post, September 30, 2021, 10:14 PM, https://twitter.com/cvaldary/status/1443757187449475072.

5. "About: Activist to Artist," Theory of Enchantment, accessed July 19, 2022, https://theoryofenchantment.com/about/.

6. Chloé S. Valdary, Twitter post, September 30, 2021, 9:58 PM, https://twitter.com/cvaldary/status/1443757187449475072.

7. Chloé S. Valdary, Twitter post, June 23, 2020, 12:12 PM, https://twitter.com/cvaldary/status/1275461728193720320.

8. Josh Packard and Casper ter Kuile, "Gen Z Is Keeping the Faith. Just Don't Expect to See Them at Worship," *National Catholic Reporter*, September 28, 2021, https://www.ncronline.org/news/opinion/gen-z-keeping-faith-just-dont-expect-see-them-worship.

9. Springtide Research Institute, "The State of Religion and Young People 2020: Catholic Edition," https://www.springtideresearch.org/research/the-state-of-religion-young-catholics.

10. Jana Riess, "Gen Z Is Lukewarm about Religion, but Open to Relationships, Study Shows," Religion News Service, December 21, 2020, https://religionnews.com/2020/12/21/gen-z-is-lukewarm-about-religion-but-open-to-relationships-study-shows/.

11. Charles C. Camosy, "Study Shows Younger People Lack Faith in Religious Institutions," *Crux*, February 17, 2021, https://cruxnow.com/interviews/2021/02/study-shows-younger-people-lack-faith-in-religious-institutions/.

12. Otis Houston, "Back into the Fold: An Interview with Chloé Valdary," *LA Review of Books*, December 12, 2019, https://lareviewofbooks.org/article/back-into-the-fold-an-interview-with-chloe-valdary/.

13. Tara Isabella Burton, "Christianity Gets Weird," *New York Times*, May 8, 2020, https://www.nytimes.com/2020/05/08/opinion/sunday/weird-christians.html.

5. The Newbie Convert

1. Kelly Johnson, "A Cradle Catholic Perspective on Converts: Theologian Converts, Part III," *Catholic Moral*

Theology, June 6, 2014, https://catholicmoraltheology. com/a-cradle-catholic-perspective-on-converts-theologian-converts-part-iii/.

2. Charles C. Camosy, "New Book Details Iranian-American's Journey to the Catholic Church," *Crux*, January 11, 2019, https://cruxnow.com/interviews/2019/01/new-book-details-iranian-americans-journey-to-the-catholic-church/.

3. Sohrab Ahmari, Twitter post, October 24, 2020, 1:41 PM, https://twitter.com/SohrabAhmari/status/1320057770473869315?s=20.

4. Sohrab Ahmari, Twitter post, October 7, 2021, 1:48 PM, https://twitter.com/SohrabAhmari/status/1446170520760815618?s=20.

5. Sohrab Ahmari, Twitter post, February 11, 2021, 9:17 AM, https://twitter.com/SohrabAhmari/status/1359869118686646272.

6. Sohrab Ahmari, "Take-Off Time for Solidarity," *American Conservative*, October 12, 2021, https://www. theamericanconservative.com/articles/ take-off-time-for-solidarity/.

7. Sohrab Ahmari, "The GOP-Corporate Divorce Is a Blessing for the Party's Future," *New York Post*, January 12, 2021, https://nypost.com/2021/01/12/the-gop-corporate-divorce-is-a-blessing-for-the-partys-future/.

8. Rick Rojas, "Becoming Catholic in the Age of Scandal," *New York Times*, May 3, 2019, https://www.nytimes.com/2019/05/03/ nyregion/converting-catholics-church-scandal.html.

9. Camosy, "New Book Details Iranian-American's Journey."

10. Johnson, "A Cradle Catholic Perspective."

6. The Single-Issue Pro-Life Activist

1. Associated Press, "Anti-Abortion Congressman Urged His Mistress to Have One, Report Says," *USA*

Today, October 3, 2017, https://www.usatoday.com/
story/news/politics/onpolitics/2017/10/03/abortion-tim-
murphy-mistress-affair/730306001/.

2. Kristen Day and Charles Camosy, "Op-Ed: How the
Democratic Platform Betrays Millions of the Party Faithful,"
LA Times, July 25, 2016, https://www.latimes.com/opinion/
op-ed/la-oe-day-and-camosy-democratic-platform-abortion-
20160725-snap-story.html.

3. Culture of Life Africa, http://cultureoflifeafrica.com/.

4. Sophia Feingold, "Pro-Life in Africa: 'What We Hold in
Common Is This Value for Family,'" *National Catholic Register*,
April 27, 2016, https://www.ncregister.com/news/pro-life-in-
africa-what-we-hold-in-common-is-this-value-for-family-
990wcul7.

5. Obianuju Ekeocha, "An African Woman's Open Letter
to Melinda Gates," Pontifical Council for the Laity, n.d., http://
www.laici.va/content/laici/en/sezioni/donna/notizie/an-afri-
can-woman-s-open-letter-to-melinda-gates.html.

6. Obianuju Ekeocha, "Neo-Colonialism and Reproductive Health," *Church Life Journal*, April 5, 2019,
https://churchlifejournal.nd.edu/articles/neo-colonialism-
and-reproductive-health/.

7. Courtney Mares, "In UN message, Pope Francis decries abortion and family breakdown," Catholic News Agency, September 25, 2020, https://www.
catholicnewsagency.com/news/45974/in-un-message-pope
z-francis-decries-abortion-and-family-breakdown.

8. Antonio Spadaro, "A Big Heart Open to God: An Interview with Pope Francis," *America*, September 30, 2013, http://
americamagazine.org/pope-interview.

9. Charles Camosy, "Does Pope Francis Have a 'Weak'
Bioethic? A Response to Mark Cherry," *Catholic Moral Theology*, February 9, 2015, http://catholicmoraltheology.com/

does-pope-francis-have-a-weak-bioethic-a-response-to-mark-cherry/.

10. Inés San Martín, "Pope Francis Once Again Enters Abortion Debate in Argentina," *Crux*, December 2, 2020, https://cruxnow.com/church-in-the-americas/2020/12/pope-francis-once-again-enters-abortion-debate-in-argentina/.

11. Quoted in Charlie Camosy, "Argentina Says the Quiet Pro-Choice Part Out Loud," *Catholic Herald*, December 30, 2020, https://catholicherald.co.uk/saying-the-pro-choice-quiet-part-out-loud/.

12. Megan Hall et al., "Associations between Intimate Partner Violence and Termination of Pregnancy: A Systematic Review and Meta-Analysis," *PLOS Medicine* 11, no. 1 (January 2014), http://www.plosmedicine.org/article/info%3Adoi%2F10.1371%2Fjournal.pmed.1001581.

13. Lyman Stone, "American Women Are Having Fewer Children Than They'd Like," *New York Times*, February 13, 2018, https://www.nytimes.com/2018/02/13/upshot/american-fertility-is-falling-short-of-what-women-want.html.

14. Press release, "Rubio, Romney Reintroduce Bill Giving New Parents Option for Paid Leave," Marco Rubio, September 15, 2021, https://www.rubio.senate.gov/public/index.cfm/2021/9/rubio-romney-reintroduce-bill-giving-new-parents-option-for-paid-leave.

15. Gallup, "Party Affiliation," n.d., https://news.gallup.com/poll/15370/party-affiliation.aspx.

16. Charles Camosy, "The GOP Tax Plan Is an Anti-Adoption Recipe for Abortion," *Washington Post*, November 7, 2017, https://www.washingtonpost.com/news/posteverything/wp/2017/11/07/the-gop-tax-plan-is-an-anti-adoption-recipe-for-abortion/.

17. "How Parents Foiled a US Republican Tax Proposal to Kill the Adoption Tax Credit," CNBC, December 1, 2017, https://www.cnbc.com/2017/12/01/

how-parents-of-adopted-children-foiled-a-us-republican-
tax-proposal.html.

7. The Progressive Professor

1. Daily Theology Podcast, "Julie Hanlon Rubio,"
April 14, 2015, https://dailytheology.org/2015/04/14/
dt-podcast-episode-1-julie-hanlon-rubio/.

2. Julie Rubio, "What If Contraception Saves Lives?"
Catholic Moral Theology, July 16, 2012, https://
catholicmoraltheology.com/what-if-contraception-saves-lives/.

3. Julie Hanlon Rubio, "In Supporting Civil Unions for
Same Sex Couples, Pope Francis Is Moving Catholics toward a
More Expansive Understanding of Family," Yahoo, November
3, 2020, https://www.yahoo.com/now/supporting-same-sex-
civil-unions-132604495.html.

4. Julie Rubio, "Symposium on Same Sex Marriage: Evolution?" Catholic Moral Theology, May 26,
2012, https://catholicmoraltheology.com/symposium
-on-same-sex-marriage-evolution/.

5. Rubio, "Symposium."

6. Julie Hanlon Rubio, *Hope for Common Ground: Mediat-
ing the Personal and the Political in a Divided Church* (Washington, DC: Georgetown University Press, 2016).

7. Julie Rubio, "A Wide Space for Prudence,"
Catholic Moral Theology, October 15, 2012, https://
catholicmoraltheology.com/a-wide-space-for-prudence/.

8. Julie Rubio, "What I Learned from Talking Economics with Libertarians," Catholic Moral Theology, May 2,
2013, https://catholicmoraltheology.com/what-i-learned-
from-talking-economics-with-libertarians/.

9. Julie Rubio, "CTSA to Theologians: Embrace Your
Conservative Colleagues," Catholic Moral Theology,
October 11, 2013, https://catholicmoraltheology.com/
ctsa-to-theologians-embrace-your-conservative-colleagues/.

10. Robert Bellarmino "Letter to Paolo A. Foscarini, on Galileo's Claim in Favor of Heliocentrism," Interdisciplinary Encyclopedia of Religion and Science, 1989, https://inters.org/Bellarmino-Letter-Foscarini.

11. Brendan Hodge, "Special Report: The Catholic Hot Buttons," The Pillar, November 12, 2021, https://www.pillarcatholic.com/p/special-report-the-catholic-hot-buttons.

12. Abigail Shrier, "Top Trans Doctors Blow the Whistle on 'Sloppy' Care," Common Sense, October 4, 2021, https://bariweiss.substack.com/p/top-trans-doctors-blow-the-whistle.

8. The Immigrant Parent

1. CARA, "The Pastoral Care of Migrants, Refugees and Travelers Worship Site Inventory and Demographic Study," June 2021, https://cara.georgetown.edu/PCMRTReport.pdf.

2. Elizabeth Podrebarac Sciupac, "Hispanic Teens Enjoy Religious Activities with Parents, but Fewer View Religion as 'Very Important,'" Pew Research Center, September 22, 2020, https://www.pewresearch.org/fact-tank/2020/09/22/hispanic-teens-enjoy-religious-activities-with-parents-but-fewer-view-religion-as-very-important/.

3. Aaron Zitner, "Hispanic Voters Now Evenly Split between Parties, WSJ Poll Finds," *Wall Street Journal*, December 8, 2021, https://www.wsj.com/articles/hispanic-voters-now-evenly-split-between-parties-wsj-poll-finds-11638972769.

4. David Crary, "In Battleground States, Catholics Are a Pivotal Swing Vote," AP News, September 22, 2020, https://apnews.com/article/election-2020-virus-outbreak-ruth-bader-ginsburg-pennsylvania-immigration-a3c8a26a15cfbe0d2eb5df225490f960.

5. José H. Gomez, *Immigration and the Next America: Renewing the Soul of Our Nation* (Huntington, IN: Our Sunday Visitor, 2013).

6. Charles C. Camosy, "In Praise of Archbishop Gómez's Anti-Racism," Religion News Service, November 12, 2021, https://religionnews.com/2021/11/12/in-praise-of-archbishop-gomezs-anti-racism/.

7. Charles C. Camosy, "Bishop Says Deporting Migrants 'Not Unlike' Abortion," *Crux*, July 27, 2016, https://cruxnow.com/interviews/2016/07/camosy-interview-bp-brownsville-tx.

8. Nichole M. Flores, *The Aesthetics of Solidarity: Our Lady of Guadalupe and American Democracy* (Washington, DC: Georgetown University Press, 2021).

9. Vivian Cabrera, "Being Family: What Latino Catholics Can Teach the Rest of the U.S. Church about Community," *America*, September 16, 2021, https://www.americamagazine.org/faith/2021/09/16/being-family-hispanic-catholics-241355.

9. The Christmas and Easter Catholic

1. Joyce Duriga, "Actor Mark Wahlberg's Faith Journey Leaves Impression on Young Adults," *Crux*, October 27, 2017, https://cruxnow.com/church-in-the-usa/2017/10/actor-mark-wahlbergs-faith-journey-leaves-impression-young-adults.

2. Eric Eisenberg, "Mark Wahlberg Apologizes to the Pope for Ted," Cinema Blend, September 27, 2015, https://www.cinemablend.com/new/Mark-Wahlberg-Apologizes-Pope-Ted-84977.html.

3. Kate Bryan, "The Secret to Mark Wahlberg's Success," Catholic Vote, October 24, 2013, https://www.catholicvote.org/the-secret-to-mark-wahlbergs-success/.

4. Cerith Gardiner, "Mark Wahlberg Reveals His Surprising Daily Prayer Routine," Aleteia, September 14, 2018, https://aleteia.org/2018/09/14/mark-wahlberg-reveals-his-surprising-daily-prayer-routine/#.

5. CARA, "Frequently Requested Church Statistics," n.d., https://cara.georgetown.edu/frequently-requested-church-statistics/.

6. Brendan Hodge, "Special Report: Who We Are, and What We Believe," The Pillar, November 8, 2021, https://www.pillarcatholic.com/p/special-report-who-we-are-and-what.

7. Mark M. Gray, "The Reverts: Catholics Who Left and Came Back," Catholic Education Resource Center, n.d., https://www.catholiceducation.org/en/controversy/common-misconceptions/the-reverts-catholics-who-left-and-came-back.html.

8. Patty Knap, "Record Numbers of Converts and Reverts 'Journey Home' to the Catholic Church," Aleteia, January 20, 2017, https://aleteia.org/2017/01/20/record-numbers-of-converts-and-reverts-journey-home-to-the-catholic-church/#.

9. The Coming Home Network International, "Revert," n.d., https://chnetwork.org/?s=revert.

10. Joyce Duriga, "Actor Mark Wahlberg's Faith Journey Leaves Impression on Young Adults," Crux, October 27, 2017, https://cruxnow.com/church-in-the-usa/2017/10/actor-mark-wahlbergs-faith-journey-leaves-impression-young-adults.

11. Gregory A. Smith, "Just One-Third of U.S. Catholics agree with Their Church that Eucharist Is Body, Blood of Christ," Pew Research Center, August 5, 2019, https://www.pewresearch.org/fact-tank/2019/08/05/transubstantiation-eucharist-u-s-catholics/.

10. The Seemingly Standoffish Parish Priest

1. "Ranking the Biggest Stars," Morning Consult, n.d., https://morningconsult.com/most-loved-entertainers/.

2. Tim Sullivan, "Father Josh: A Married Catholic Priest in a Celibate World," AP News, February 17, 2020, https://apnews.com/article/ap-top-news-us-news-dallas-pope-francis-religion-14c50cda5f6430f56420efd14058624e.

3. Conor McDonough, Twitter post, December 24, 2021, 4:47 AM, https://twitter.com/ConorMcDonough4/status/1474315731445719041?t=AdA_SwoDVLkCPvp-pLWqYpQ&s=03.

4. CARA, "Enter by the Narrow Gate: Satisfaction and Challenges among Recently Ordained Priests," n.d., https://cara.georgetown.edu/wp-content/uploads/2020/11/NACTS.pdf.

5. Jim McDermott, "Dear Bishops: We Need to Talk about the Crisis of Despair in Catholic Priests," *America*, November 15, 2021, https://www.americamagazine.org/faith/2021/11/15/priest-survey-despair-241838.

6. Charles C. Camosy, "National Vocations Week and the Problem of 'Dissatisfied' Priests," *Crux*, November 8, 2021, https://cruxnow.com/interviews/2021/11/national-vocations-week-and-the-problem-of-dissatisfied-priests.

7. John Cavadini, "Co-Responsibility: An Antidote to Clericalizing the Laity?" *Church Life Journal*, March 26, 2020, https://churchlifejournal.nd.edu/articles/co-responsibility-is-the-remedy-for-lay-clericalism/.

8. "Address of His Holiness Benedict XVI, Opening of the Pastoral Convention of the Diocese of Rome on the Theme: 'Church Membership and Pastoral Co-Responsibility,'" May 26, 2009, http://www.vatican.va/content/benedict-xvi/en/speeches/2009/may/documents/hf_ben-xvi_spe_20090526_convegno-diocesi-rm.html.

Conclusion

1. David French, "We Argue in All the Wrong Ways," *The Atlantic*, November 24, 2021, https://newsletters.theatlantic.com/the-third-rail/619e96e531249e0022c34406/we-argue-in-all-the-wrong-ways/.

2. "History," Our Lady Undoer of Knots, n.d., http://www.maryundoerofknots.com/history.htm.

3. "Pope Francis Turns to Mary, Undoer of Knots, at End of Rosary Marathon for End to Pandemic," Catholic News Agency, May 31, 2021, https://www.catholicnewsagency.com/news/247848/pope-francis-turns-to-mary-undoer-of-knots-at-end-of-rosary-marathon-for-end-to-pandemic.

Charles C. Camosy is a professor at the Creighton University School of Medicine and the Msgr. Curran Fellow in Moral Theology at St. Joseph Seminary in New York. He is a columnist for Religion News Service, the *Angelus*, and the *Pillar*.

Camosy is the author of eight books, including the award-winning *Too Expensive to Treat?*, *Peter Singer and Christian Ethics*, and *Beyond the Abortion Wars*. Camosy's book, *For Love of Animals* was featured in the *New York Times*. He is the founding editor of The Magenta Project series and the founding director of the Catholic Conversation Project.

Camosy earned bachelor's and master's degrees from the University of Notre Dame, where he also received his doctorate.

His writing has been featured in publications including the *American Journal of Bioethics*, the *Journal of the Catholic Health Association*, the *New York Times*, the *Washington Post*, the *New York Daily News*, the *Los Angeles Times*, *Church Life Journal*, *Commonweal*, *America* magazine, *Crux*, the *Tablet*, and the *National Catholic Reporter*. Camosy serves as a mortal theology consultant for *Busted Halo*. He is an advisor for the faith outreach office of the Humane Society of the United States, the pro-life commission of the Archdiocese of New York, and Holy Name Medical Center. He received the Robert Bryne award from the Fordham Respect Life Club and the 2018 St. Jerome Award for scholarly excellence from the Catholic Library Association.

Camosy and his family live in West Orange, New Jersey.

charlescamosy.com
Facebook: Charlie.Camosy
Twitter: @ccamosy

AVE MARIA PRESS

Founded in 1865, Ave Maria Press,
a ministry of the Congregation of
Holy Cross, is a Catholic publishing
company that serves the spiritual and
formative needs of the Church and its
schools, institutions, and ministers;
Christian individuals and families; and
others seeking spiritual nourishment.

For a complete listing of titles from

Ave Maria Press

Sorin Books

Forest of Peace

Christian Classics

visit www.avemariapress.com

AVE MARIA PRESS
Notre Dame, IN
A Ministry of the United States Province of Holy Cross